A CONCI
TO W

by
R. A. PENFOLD

BERNARD BABANI (publishing) LTD
THE GRAMPIANS
SHEPHERDS BUSH ROAD
LONDON W6 7NF
ENGLAND

Please Note

Although every care has been taken with the production of this book to ensure that any projects, designs, modifications and/or programs etc. contained herewith, operate in a correct and safe manner and also that any components specified are normally available in Great Britain, the Publishers and Author do not accept responsibility in any way for the failure, including fault in design, of any project, design, modification or program to work correctly or to cause damage to any other equipment that it may be connected to or used in conjunction with, or in respect of any other damage or injury that may be so caused, nor do the Publishers accept responsibility in any way for the failure to obtain specified components.

Notice is also given that if equipment that is still under warranty is modified in any way or used or connected with home-built equipment then that warranty may be void.

© 1989 BERNARD BABANI (publishing) LTD

First Published — November 1989
Revised and Reprinted — October 1991

British Library Cataloguing in Publication Data:
Penfold, R. A.
    A concise introduction to Wordperfect.
    1. Word processing. Software packages, Wordperfect
    I. Title
    652'.5'028553

ISBN 0 85934 207 7

Printed and Bound in Great Britain by Cox & Wyman Ltd, Reading

Preface

Wordperfect has now become the most popular word processor for the IBM PC range and the numerous "compatibles" in use around the world. In fact it must rank as one of the most successful pieces of software ever produced, with hundreds of thousands of users. Although the majority of users are running Wordperfect on an IBM PC or a "clone", it is also available in versions for many other computers, including the Atari ST series and the Commodore Amiga range. As far as possible, the features of various versions, the command structures, and even the key codes needed to access a particular function, have been kept the same. If you learn to use Wordperfect on one computer, changing to a different computer should give few problems.

The main reasons for Wordperfect's success are almost certainly its speed of operation and the vast range of features it offers. It has to be asked to do a large task before it keeps you waiting for a significant amount of time, and I have never managed to out-type it. Its features include a comprehensive mail-merge facility for customising standard letters etc., a spelling checker, a thesaurus, a very capable sort routine and some very impressive formatting capabilities (probably limited more by your printer than the program).

The problem with any full-feature word processor is that it inevitably takes a fair amount of learning effort in order to master the general inputting of text, formatting, printing and the more advanced features that you require. This book does not set out to be a complete course covering every aspect of Wordperfect, which is something that would probably require several books of this size. However, it will teach you the basics of getting your documents into Wordperfect, formatting them, and getting them printed out. It also covers most of Wordperfect's major features, including mail-merge and graphics.

Since originally writing this book, the latest version of Wordperfect 5.1 has become available. This is largely compatible with earlier versions, particularly version 5.0. It mainly adds features to Wordperfect 5.0 rather than making any radical changes to the command structure. Therefore, the information provided in Chapters 1, 2 and 3 applies to version 5.1 as well as version 5.0. By now including Chapter 4 we can look at some of the main additions in Wordperfect 5.1.

R. A. Penfold

Trademarks

MS-DOS is a registered trademark of Microsoft Corporation.

IBM, PC, XT, and **AT** are registered trademarks of International Business Machines Corporation.

Wordperfect is a registered trademark of the Wordperfect Corporation.

Atari and **ST** are registered trademarks of the Atari Corporation.

Amiga is a trademark of Commodore-Amiga Inc.

Contents

Chapter 1

GETTING STARTED

Word processing is an application to which microcomputers are well suited, and it is not surprising that this is one of the earliest uses to which they were put. By comparison with a modern up-market word processor like Wordperfect, running on a powerful modern microcomputer, most of the early word processors were rather crude. A spelling checker with a large vocabulary is a standard item these days, but was not available on the early word processing programs, except perhaps, as a stand-alone program to process files produced by the word processor. Something not really comparable to the integrated spelling checker of Wordperfect.

Probably the biggest problem with early word processor software was that it was difficult to use. Modern software in general is much more "user friendly" than software of a few years ago, but this is to some extent offset by the vast range of features offered by most programs. Each command is reasonably easy to use, but there are so many facilities that it is difficult to learn exactly what each one does, and how it is used.

Research suggests that most users only utilize 10 to 20% of their word processor's capabilities. I suppose this would seem to suggest that most users greatly under utilize their word processor. This is probably not a very realistic way of looking at things though. Most users utilize only a moderate percentage of the available word processor features because that is all they require for their particular application. Although it might appear that a simple word processor would suit the requirements of most users, this is probably incorrect. You need a word processor that provides the right features, and this probably means having to buy a complex piece of software that includes all the features you require amongst its vast array of facilities. You might be lucky enough to find a simple and low cost program that just happens to have all the functions you require, but this has to be regarded as something of an outside chance.

The Right Approach

The implication of all this for someone trying to come to grips with a program such as Wordperfect is that they should not try to go through the manual learning all about every available function.

1

Doing this will at best result in a lot of learning effort directed at parts of the program that are never likely to be utilized in earnest. At worst there is a risk of getting really bogged down and giving up. The best approach is almost certainly that of learning some of the fundamentals of using the program (cursor control, printing, etc.), and then going quickly through the list of features to find those that are likely to be of real use to you. Your learning effort can then be directed towards the features that you will really need in practice.

The purpose of this book is not to teach everything you will ever need to know about Wordperfect. As the size of the Wordperfect manual testifies, a large book is needed in order to cover everything in fairly cursory fashion. A detailed explanation of all aspects of the program would require several large books! This book is aimed first at making it as easy as possible to get started with Wordperfect. The first part of this chapter covers the things you really must know in order to use the program. The rest of the chapter describes some of the more minor but useful facilities of Wordperfect. Chapter 2 covers the installation of printer drivers, and getting documents printed out in the required format. You need to understand a fair amount of the material in both chapters before you start using Wordperfect in earnest to produce anything other than short and simple documents. Chapter 3 covers the more major features of the program, such as the spelling checker, thesaurus, sort and mail-merge function. These are non-essential facilities, but ones that can be very useful to people producing certain types of document.

Most of the features that the majority of users will require are covered in this book, and some commands are covered in much more detail than others. For details of the more esoteric features of the program you will need to study the manual. However, once you have mastered the main functions of the program and become familiar with the general way in which commands are organised, learning to operate the more obscure commands is reasonably easy.

Wordperfect Versions

It is assumed here that the user has Wordperfect up and running. We will not be concerned with getting the program loaded onto a hard disk etc., which is all covered in some detail in the Wordperfect documentation. It is also assumed that the user is familiar with the basics of MS/DOS, or whatever operating system the computer is running under, and the fundamentals of computers, disks, etc. If you are not familiar with any of these subjects, there are plenty of books available that will provide the information you require. Learning about these aspects of computing is not particularly difficult, and in order to run applications software successfully you need only a very superficial knowledge of them.

One slight complication is that there is more than one version of Wordperfect in use   Version 4.1 was the start of Wordperfect as we know it today, but most users have now progressed to versions 4.2 or 5.0.   The differences between versions 4.1 and 4.2 are not vast. Wordperfect 5.0 introduced some major new features, but it mainly differs from earlier versions in that it provides some graphics support. As far as the text functions are concerned, it is very similar to the earlier versions, although there are differences in the way in which some commands operate.   The printing of documents for instance, is handled somewhat differently in version 5.0.

There is a further complication in that Wordperfect is in use on a variety of computers.   Probably the vast majority of Wordperfect users are running the program on an IBM PC or compatible computer, but this program is also used a great deal by Atari ST, Commodore Amiga, and Apple Macintosh owners, and is also available for some other computers.   Although version 5.0 is available for the IBM PCs and compatibles, at the time of writing this version 4.2 is the most up-to-date version available for most of the other computers.

There are slight differences in the commands depending on the version you have and the computer you are running. In this book we will mainly be concerned with version 5.0 on the IBM PCs, but where version 4.2 is substantially different this will be pointed out.

In most cases the way in which commands are used under version 4.2 is not vastly different (or is the same), and versions for different computers are made as similar as possible by the Wordperfect programmers.   This book should be usable with versions 4.1, 4.2, or 5.0 running on any computer, but you need to be aware that there might be some differences in the menus and menu structures described in this book and those of your program if you are using anything other than version 5.0 running on an IBM PC compatible of some kind.   The "Quick Reference" chart supplied with Wordperfect should enable you to quickly locate any command that requires a different key sequence.   If you are using a version of Wordperfect other than those mentioned above (or something

3

beyond version 5.0 if this should come along in due course), then this book might be of limited use to you.

It should perhaps be explained that the IBM PC versions of Wordperfect do not have any mouse support. The only way of accessing commands is by pressing the right keyboard key or keys. In fact some IBM PC mice are supplied with software to provide Wordperfect with pop-down menus, or with software that enables the user to produce his or her own menus for applications programs such as Wordperfect. A mouse and menus represent an easy way of operating a complex program initially, but can make things a bit slow and tedious in the long term. A mouse is something less than ideal for a program such as a word processor where you really need both hands to operate the keyboard. In this book we will only be concerned about accessing commands and menus via the keyboard, but if your computer and version of Wordperfect have mouse support, you can of course access commands by way of the mouse and pop-down menus if preferred.

The Bottom Line
When you run the Wordperfect program you are initially greeted with a largely blank screen. This is sometimes put forward as a criticism of the program, but it should really be regarded as an asset. The usual 80 column by 25 line (or thereabouts) computer text display does not really show a great deal at once. The full screen can only display something less than half an A4 page of text. Using up a large proportion of the screen on status information, help information, etc., can leave so little of the screen left for the document you are working on that life becomes difficult, with a lot of scrolling up and down through the document every time you need to refer back to something.

The bottom line of the display includes some basic information which is all you will normally need to know. At the left hand side of this line the name of the current document is displayed. This will initially be blank, but it will automatically display the name of the document when you load one from disk, or type one into the computer and save it to disk.

On the right hand side of the status line some basic information about where you are in the document is displayed. First this tells you which document you are currently editing (1 or 2). Wordperfect enables you to have two documents loaded into the program, but you would normally only have one or the other displayed at any one time (split screen operation is possible though, as described later). The next section tells you the current page number. Note that Wordperfect does not operate on the basis of having pages as separate screens of text. The text is effectively in one long screenful, and you can scroll vertically through the text to display the section you require. Broken lines across the screen show the boundaries between pages. What these page break lines are showing you is how the document will be broken up into pages when it is printed out. Until the document is printed out these page breaks are notional rather than real.

The next, and final two sections of the status line show the position of the cursor on the page. Again, the page position is with reference to the printed document, and not the screen position. It shows the position in terms of the distance down from the top of the page, and the distance in from the left hand edge of the page. The cursor incidentally, is an on-screen character of some kind. The standard Wordperfect cursor is a flashing underline character. The cursor shows where any text typed into a document will appear, or where any action in general will occur. Note that in versions 4.1 and 4.2 of Wordperfect the cursor position is shown in terms of lines down from the top of the page, and characters in from the left hand side of the page.

A slight change occurs in the status line if you press the "Insert" key. The document name at the left hand end of the line should be replaced with the word "Typeover". Pressing "Insert" again will cause the status line to return to normal, pressing this key again will result in the word "Typeover" appearing again, and so on. Normally Wordperfect is in the "insert" mode. This means that any text you type in will be added to the existing text. The "insert" key enables you to switch between the "insert" and "typeover" modes. In computer terminology, you use this key to "toggle" between these two modes. In the "Typeover" mode, text typed into the computer will replace any text at the cursor position. When the cursor is at the end of a document there is no difference between the two modes. If you place the cursor in the middle of some text, and start typing while the program is in the "Insert" mode, the new text will be added into the middle of the existing text. Any text below or to the right of the cursor will automatically be shifted down and along to make way for the new text. In the "Typeover" mode, existing text stays in place, and is overwritten by any new text that you type in.

Many word processors are normally in the "Typeover" mode, and are only switched to the "Insert" mode when absolutely necessary. In my opinion at any rate, defaulting to the "Insert" mode (as in Wordperfect) is a better way of doing things. It reduces the risk of accidentally typing over text that you wish to retain, and when editing a document you mostly need to add extra text. Typing over old text and replacing it with new material is something that you will probably only need to do relatively infrequently. Even where this should prove to be necessary, it might be safer and easier to first delete the unwanted text, and to then add the new material using the "Insert" mode.

The apparent reason for some word processors not encouraging use of the "Insert" mode is that they operate very slowly when used in this way. You can tend to find that the program is lagging well behind what you have typed in, and with some word processors I have tried there was even a problem with characters being missed out. Wordperfect operates very quickly, and I have never managed to out-type it even when running it on a relatively slow computer. To some extent this speed is achieved by not totally reformatting the text as each new character is added. As a result of this, the text is not properly formatted as you type in new text. This does not really matter, since everything springs into place as soon as you finish typing and start to move the cursor to a new position.

Entering Text
The cursor can be moved around a document in a number of ways, but it is basically controlled by the four cursor keys, which can be used in conjunction with certain other keys in order to rapidly move the cursor by large amounts. The cursor keys are the four which are marked with arrows pointing up, down, left, and right. The arrow indicates the direction in which the key moves the cursor. If your computer has an 84 key IBM style keyboard, the cursor keys are part of the numeric keypad towards the right hand end of the keyboard. The "Num Lock" key toggles the keypad between numeric and cursor operation. The "Num Lock" indicator light is switched on when the keypad is in the numeric mode. If this light is switched on you will need to press the "Num Lock" key in order to switch out the indicator light and set the keypad for cursor control. Most computers are set up so that the keypad defaults to cursor control at switch-on.

Do not panic if the cursor controls seem to have no effect. They only permit the cursor to be moved within the confines of the document. Wordperfect differs from some other word processors in this respect. There are advantages in being able to move the cursor anywhere without any restraints, and there are advantages in the Wordperfect method. Quite frankly, it does not matter a great deal, and you should soon be able to get used to either method.

In order to try out the cursor controls, type some lines of text into the computer. In fact to fully try out the methods of cursor control you should type in a few pages of text. You may prefer to type in a few lines of text, and then refer to the section on block copying. This will enable you to repeatedly copy the initial lines of text so that you can quickly put together a few pages of text so that you can experiment with the cursor controls. You should soon get the hang of controlling the cursor using the four cursor keys, and you are then ready to try the quick methods of moving the cursor.

If you press the "Home" key followed by one of the cursor keys, you will find that the cursor jumps as far as possible in the direction dictated by the cursor key you operate. For example, if you press "Home" and the "up" cursor key, the cursor will move to the top line of the screen. This feature is especially useful when you are checking through and correcting a document. Scrolling up through a document places the cursor at the bottom of the screen, but you will often notice errors at or close to the top line of the display. Pressing "Home" and the "up" cursor key provides an almost instant means of moving the cursor to the appropriate area of the screen. Pressing "Home" and then the "down" cursor key enables the cursor to be quickly moved back to the bottom line of the screen so that you can scroll up through the document again. Note that you do not need to simultaneously hold down the "Home" key and one of the cursor keys. You press and release "Home", after which you press and release the appropriate cursor key.

Another very useful feature of Wordperfect is the ability to quickly go to the beginning or end of a document. I have encountered a few word processor programs where it was only possible to get from the beginning to the end of a document (or vice versa) by scrolling (often quite slowly) through the entire document. With Wordperfect, in order to move from any point in the document to its end you simply press "Home" twice followed by the "down" cursor key. To move from any point in the document to its beginning you simply press "Home" twice followed by the "up" cursor key.

The "Pg Up" (Page Up) and "Pg Dn" (Page Down) keys do precisely what their names imply. Operating one of these moves the cursor up or down by one page. This description is not strictly accurate, since this method of cursor movement does not necessarily shift the cursor up or down by precisely one page. It moves the cursor to the first line in the previous or subsequent page. The "End" key simply moves the cursor to the right hand end of the current line. It gives the same effect as pressing "Home" and the "right" cursor key, but is quicker since it only requires a single key press.

Cursor movement along a line can be quite slow using the "left" and "right" cursor keys, the speed of movement depending on which version of the program and which computer you are using. Movement can be speeded up by pressing "Ctrl" and one of these cursor keys. This moves the cursor one word at a time rather than character by character. Finally, pressing "Ctrl" and "Home" accesses the "Go To" facility. Type the required page number and then press the "Return" key, and Wordperfect will move the cursor to the specified page.

Deleting

I suppose that one of the biggest advantages of a word processor over a typewriter is the ease with which unwanted text can be deleted. You get everything just right on the screen first, and only then commit the text to paper via the printer. There are two keys which can be used for deleting text. One of these is marked "del" or "delete", and this is duplicated on the 101/102 key IBM PC style keyboards. It is present in the bottom row of the numeric keypad, as well as in the cluster of six keys to the left of this keypad. In fact the "Insert", "Home", "Page Up", "Page Down", "End" and "Delete" keys are all duplicated in this cluster of six keys. These keys will always function properly, whether "Num Lock" is on or off (as will the four cursor keys beneath them). The equivalent keys in the numeric keypad will operate as number keys if "Num Lock" is on.

The "delete" key removes the character at the current cursor position, if there is one. If the cursor is at the end of the document, pressing "delete" has no effect. If the cursor is in the middle of some text, pressing "delete" removes the character above the cursor, and the character to right of the cursor moves one place to the left to take the place of the deleted character. In fact a lot of the text to the right of the cursor and below it might move in order to keep everything neat and tidy when text is deleted from anywhere other than the end of a document. In the interest of speed, Wordperfect does not reformat the whole document as each character is removed. However, any raggedness in the text should be rapidly sorted out when you have finished deleting and the cursor is moved.

The second form of delete key is the backspace one. This is usually at the top right hand corner of the main cluster of keys, and it is often just marked with an arrow pointing towards the left. Pressing this key removes the character one position before the cursor. This is normally the character immediately to the left of the cursor, but if it is at the beginning of a line, then it is the last character on the line above that will be deleted. A lot of deleting is necessary because you have just typed something that is incorrect, or you wish to change it for some reason, and the backspace key usually receives a fair amount of use.

Repeats

Bear in mind that most keys have an auto-repeat facility. This is where holding a key down causes the appropriate character to be repeatedly typed onto the screen for you until the key is released. This facility operates with both forms of delete key, and you can quickly remove a number of words in this way. Be careful though, as the auto-repeat facility works quite fast on some computers, and with one of these you can easily delete a bit more than you intended to. With several word processors I have used there has been a tendency for the program to lag behind the keyboard somewhat when using the auto-repeat for deleting. You hold down the delete or backspace key until you have removed all the unwanted text, release the key, and then watch as the computer continues to delete text for a few more seconds! Fortunately, I have never experienced this problem with Wordperfect, which always seems to be able to keep up with the keyboard.

Note that if you wish to remove more than about one line of text, using the block delete facility will almost certainly be quicker, and will certainly be less tedious than using auto-repeat with one of the delete keys. Block operations are covered later in this chapter.

You may from time to time delete something and then change your mind. Wordperfect has what is generally called an "undelete" facility, or what in Wordperfect terminology is a "Cancel" facility. This is accessed by pressing function key "F1". If you are using an IBM 101/102 style keyboard (or similar), the functions keys are twelve keys in the top row. On the IBM 84 key layout the function keys are the ten keys grouped together at the left hand side of the keyboard. Wordperfect is sometimes criticised for its use of the functions keys to call up the required function, as it can be difficult to remember which key or combination of keys has the desired effect. Many other programs use the letter keys in conjunction with the control ("Ctrl") and alternate ("Alt") keys to call up functions. For instance, the undelete facility could be called up using the "Ctrl" and "U" keys.

This second method can make it easier to remember the appropriate key presses for the functions you require, but it is still quite difficult to learn a large number of key codes using this method. The Wordperfect method is to use the function keys plus the control, alternate and the shift keys in order to call up the required functions. To make things easier for newcomers to the program, it is supplied complete with a plastic template which fits above or around the function keys, depending on the type of keyboard you are using. Many experienced Wordperfect users leave this template permanently in place and beginners should certainly have it fitted to the keyboard whenever running Wordperfect.

Returning to the undeleting of text, try typing in some text, deleting some of it and then pressing function key one ("F1"). The status line at the bottom of the screen will change, with the name of the document (if any) being replaced with something like "Undelete: 1 Restore; 2 Previous Deletion:". Also, the text you just deleted should reappear on the screen, but it will be made to stand out from the main text in some way. It might be in a different colour, or in reverse video for example. In order to restore the text you just removed, press the "1" key. Note that to select the desired function from a list of options, it is the appropriate numeric key that you must operate, not the function key of that number.

The undelete facility of Wordperfect is quite advanced, and it remembers the last three deletions. Try typing in some text, and deleting three words at different points in the text. If you then press "F1", you will again be presented with the undelete message at the bottom of the screen, together with the last word you deleted.

Instead of pressing "1" to restore the last deletion, select "Previous Deletion:" by pressing the "2" key. This should result in the second word you deleted being shown on screen in place of the last word deleted. Pressing "2" again will result in this word being replaced by the first word you deleted, and a third press on "2" will take things back to the beginning with the last deletion being displayed again.

By pressing "2" until the required text is displayed, and then selecting "Restore" by pressing "1", you can undelete any of the last three deletions. However, there is a slight catch here which must be avoided. Although the text removed by the last three deletions is stored in the computer's memory, their position in the text is not. As you will discover if you try out this command, the restored text is placed in the document at the current cursor position. Therefore, in order to properly restore any deleted text you must move the cursor to the correct starting position for that text.

Although Wordperfect has commands for moving and copying text, it is sometimes quicker and easier to use the delete and undelete functions for this purpose. I often use this method if I only need to move a small amount of text. Suppose for example, that you decide that the text would read better if two sentences were to be swopped over. To do this you could delete the first sentence, move the cursor to the end of the second sentence, and then press "F1" and "1" to restore the first sentence to its new position. If you wish to place a sentence at several points in a document, it can be deleted, immediately restored again if it is required at that position in the document, and then restored at other points in the text after moving the cursor to the appropriate positions in the text. Undeleting some text does not remove that text from the undelete command. The text remains in the computer's memory and can be restored as many times as you wish, wherever in the document you like!

Exiting

From time to time you will inevitably enter a Wordperfect command but change your mind and wish to do nothing. Also, you will probably accidentally select the wrong command from time to time. Some commands take effect as soon as you hit the appropriate key or keys. These are mostly things such as switching to underlined text, where no text is underlined until you type in some text. Commands of this type have a toggle action where pressing the right key or keys selects them, and using the same key code again switches them off. Thus, if you select a function of this type by mistake, you can simply use the same key or key combination again in order to switch it off.

Many Wordperfect commands provide on-screen prompts, and you are required to select the required option by pressing the appropriate number key. These prompts are often on the status line, but in some cases there are too many to fit onto one line, and the document display will be replaced with a menu screen. Do not panic if this happens — your text is safe and is restored to the screen as soon as you finish using the command. It is usually possible to get out of a menu screen by selecting the "Exit" option. This might not be shown on the menu as an option, but usually hitting the "0" key switches back to the document screen. Normally you will see that a "0" is displayed above the cursor, and this will be used as the default if you press the "Return" key. Therefore, if you get into a menu screen by accident, simply pressing the "Return" key will usually get you out of it. Try selecting the undelete function, and then press "Return". Before pressing "Return" you should notice the "0" above the cursor, and having pressed it you should return to the document which should show no changes resulting from the undelete command.

There are two further means of getting out of commands without having to go through with them. These are to press the "Esc" ("Escape") or "F7" keys. The actions of these two keys are often the same, but there are differences in some cases. In particular, having gone into a menu screen, some commands then take you into sub-menus, or possibly even sub-sub-menus. Operating "F7" usually takes you back to the document screen immediately. Using the "Esc" key usually only takes you back to the previous menu. Sometimes you may find that "Esc" has no effect but "F7" should then take you out of the command. Getting right out of a command can therefore take several pushes of the "Esc" key, and in some cases you might even need to hit "F7" several times in order to exit from deep into a string of sub-menus. If you get into trouble, repeatedly pressing "Esc" and (or) "F7" should always get you back to the main document screen.

Save and Load
If you press "F7" when you are not in a command, Wordperfect will assume that you wish to exit from the program and back to the

operating system. Before exiting from the program you will be asked to confirm that you really wish to do so. This is a safety measure which ensures that you will not exit from the program if you should accidentally hit the "F7" key. Remember that once you have gone back into the operating system, the document you were working on is effectively wiped from the computer's memory. If you go straight back into the program you will be greeted with a blank screen. As a point of interest, Wordperfect will usually ask for confirmation that a command should be carried out. if that command is a type which will drastically affect the document (a block delete for example). Pressing the "Y" key confirms that the command should be executed, or pressing the "N" key aborts the command.

In order to store documents for future editing or printing sessions you must save them to disk. It is standard practice to save work to disk (say) every fifteen minutes when you are working on a long document. If there should be a power failure, or an equipment failure, you could find yourself in the position where the document in memory is lost. The disk file may not contain all of the document, but it will at least limit the loss to no more than a few minutes work. Disks are very reliable, but it is sensible to take two disk copies of long or important documents just in case the disk is faulty, the drive is not writing to it correctly, or one copy should become damaged in some way.

If you have a computer that is fitted with a hard disk drive the standard method of working is to save the document to the hard disk while you are working on it. When the document is complete or you have finished working on it for the time being, it is saved to the hard disk, and then to a floppy disk. With a floppy drive system you can use much the same system, but with the document being saved to two separate floppy disks. You could in fact save the document to the same floppy disk under two different names, but this is a rather risky way of doing things. A fault which affects one file on the disk may well affect the other. Similarly, any damage to the disk is quite likely to render both copies of the document unreadable by the disk drive.

In order to save a document to disk you simply press "F10", and you will then be prompted at the status line to give the name under which the document must be stored on disk. This name must conform to the restrictions imposed by the operating system. For an IBM compatible computer running under PC or MS/DOS this means that the main file name must be no more than eight characters long. A three character "extension" is allowed, and this is separated from the main file name by a fullstop (" . "). Any letters and numbers can be used in the main file name and the extension, but few other characters are allowed. However, you can use the underline (" _ ") character. MS/DOS and most other operating systems do not differentiate between upper and lower case letters. Consequently, a file name such as "DOCUMENT" is no different to the file name "document" as far as the computer is concerned.

Some programs automatically add a three letter extension to file names in order to show which program has produced the file. Wordperfect does not do this, and will leave off the extension unless you specifically add one when asked to supply a file name. It can be useful to use extensions on file names as they can make it easier to locate the required file from a list of files on disk, and it can also make it easier when using the operating system for such tasks as selectively copying or deleting files. You could, for instance, use the extension ".let" for letters, ".inv" for invoices, ".ack" for acknowledgements, and so on. In many cases there may be no point in using extensions, and I never bother to do so. This is really something that depends on the type of word processing applications you will be involved in, and is something you must decide for yourself. If you do make use of extensions, be careful to avoid the ones that the operating system uses for special types of file. For instance, with a program running under MS/DOS it is advisable to avoid the extensions ".BAT", ".SYS", ".EXE", and ".COM".

Wordperfect stores your document files on the disk in which the Wordperfect program itself resides, unless that is, you direct it to do otherwise. If the program disk has sub-directories, and Wordperfect is in one of these sub-directories, by default your document files will be stored in the sub-directory in which the Wordperfect program resides. If you are running Wordperfect from a hard disk it will usually be in a sub-directory called "WP", or perhaps "WP5" if you are running version 5.0 of Wordperfect.

You may be content to save document files to the default disk and directory, but in practice you will probably wish to save them elsewhere on occasions. As a couple of examples, if you have a hard disk system but wish to save files to backup floppy disks, you will need to redirect the output of the save command to a floppy disk drive. With a hard disk system it is often convenient if files are stored in groups, with each group being in its own sub-directory or sub-sub-directory. All the files for this book, for instance, are in a sub-directory of the Wordperfect sub-directory called "WPBK".

To redirect the output of the save command to the root directory of a different disk, simply add the disk drive letter plus a colon ahead of the file name. As an example, to save the file "document" to drive A instead of the Wordperfect sub-directory on hard disk C, the file name would be given as "A:document". To save this file on drive C, but in a sub-directory of the Wordperfect sub-directory called "letters", the file name would be given as "C:\wp\letters\document". Note that there is no space between the drive identification and the filename (or anywhere else in the file name and path). Note also that the "separator" used between each section of the file name is the " \ " character, not the more familiar " / " backslash character.

Once a document has been saved under a particular path and file name, that name will appear at the left hand section of the status line. This then becomes the default which will be used in any further save commands, but if you should over-ride the default, the new path and name you supply will then become the default. This can be inconvenient at times, but usually it will save some typing, particularly if you make a lot of use of sub-directories, and sub-directories branching out from sub-directories.

If you try to save an updated version of a document using the same file name that was used for the old version, you will be asked whether or not you wish to replace the existing file. Press the "Y" key if you wish to do so, or the "N" key if you do not. If you press "N", you will be prompted for a new file name. I usually just keep saving each version of a document under the same file name. This is slightly risky in that should a fault develop while a new version is being written to the disk, you could end up in the position where you do not have a readable copy of the file on the disk. There is less risk of this happening if you save new versions of the document under new file names. On the other hand, this can quickly lead to the situation where disks rapidly fill up with a bewildering number of files. Possibly the best method would be to use two file names, and to alternate between the two. This would leave the previous version of a file safely on the disk if something should happen to go wrong while saving the current version. It limits the number of files to just two per document.

My standard method of ending a session after working on a long Wordperfect document is to first use the save command ("F10") to save the document to the hard disk. Then I use the exit command to save the document to a floppy disk in drive A and exit from the program. It is possible to use the "F7" key to exit from the current document, but not from the program. In other words, you can use this command to finish work on one document and start another. Simply press "F7" and answer "Y" if you wish to save the current document to disk. Once you have done this, or pressed "N" if you do not wish to save the current document, you will be asked something along the lines "Exit From Program? Y/N". If you answer "Y" the program is terminated and you are placed back into the operating system. If you answer "N" the current document is cleared from the screen and the computer's memory, and you are ready to commence the next document.

Loading, Etc.

Wordperfect offers three methods of loading an existing file ready for you to recommence work on it. One method is to add the name of the document after "wp" when you run the program (remembering to add a space between "wp" and the file name). From within Wordperfect, once the program is up and running, the "Retrieve" command can be used. This is initiated by pressing first the "Shift" key, and then "F10" while still holding down the shift key. When using any Wordperfect command that requires two keys to be operated, you should always press "Ctrl", "Alt", or the "Shift" key first, and hold it down while pressing the appropriate function key. The "Retrieve" command will prompt you for the file name, and this must include the correct disk identification, path and extension where appropriate.

The third alternative is to invoke the "List Files" command by pressing "F5". This will bring up a prompt at the left hand end of the status line showing the default disk drive and path name where appropriate. You will also see "*.*" at the end of this section of the status line. This simply indicates that Wordperfect will list all files on the specified disk, or in the specified directory. You can type in a different disk drive identification and path name if required, and select only certain files for display. For example, if you only wanted files having "LET" as the extension to be displayed, the final part file name/path would be changed from "*.*" to "*.LET".

When any necessary changes to the drive, file name, path and filter have been made, pressing the "Return" key will produce a list

Document size: 0   Free: 1271808   Used: 2077822

<CURRENT>	<DIR>			<PARENT>	<DIR>		
CMBK .	<DIR>	28/02/89	00:12	DABK .	<DIR>	20/12/88	23:51
MIDI .	<DIR>	19/01/89	10:25	MMBK .	<DIR>	13/05/89	05:51
WPBK .	<DIR>	26/04/89	07:18	A .	1219	03/01/89	00:48
AAFSINOS.	4668	14/01/89	23:57	ADDON .	7806	20/01/89	00:13
ADI1_89	16038	26/01/89	00:58	ADI5_B9	10792	21/05/89	22:39
ADIFINSH.	12345	23/06/89	00:58	ADIHTSNK.	16996	24/04/89	22:39
ADIPRELM.	13509	28/03/89	00:45	AFSINOSC.	5176	14/01/89	23:41
ALLOPHNS.	8770	13/04/89	02:59	ASTTURBO.FRS	3976	03/05/89	06:15
BBC1MBUS.	12912	29/03/89	07:27	BBCAUTOF.	11055	24/01/89	02:12
BBCBUS3	15770	25/05/89	00:02	BBCBUS4 .	12369	26/06/89	21:58
BBCRECAP.	11913	28/02/89	03:01	BEEBBUS2.	14721	22/04/89	22:49
BSLTTR	2425	08/06/89	01:39	CHKKBLRB.	1616	21/02/89	02:04
CHEKINDX.	5897	10/02/89	22:44	CMOSPRBE.	6204	03/04/89	21:33
COMPMUSY.	2523	21/12/88	12:38	COMPS .	2009	10/04/89	11:23
COMPS1	3995	04/04/89	11:54	COMPS2 .	3455	04/04/89	10:18
COMPS3	3377	04/04/89	12:08	COVBLURB.	1911	11/01/89	05:13
CPCSPCH	21805	15/04/89	22:31	DIYPCS	31187	20/06/89	09:02
EGA512 .FRS	3584	01/11/88	11:29	EGAITAL .FRS	3584	01/11/88	11:29

1 Retrieve; 2 Delete; 3 Move/Rename; 4 Print; 5 Text In;
6 Look; 7 Other Directory; 8 Copy; 9 Word Search; N Name Search: 6

Fig. 1.1 An example "List Files" screen. The central screen area can be scrolled to show details of further files in the sub-directory or disk.

17

of all the appropriate files that Wordperfect can locate (as in the example of Figure 1.1). These are shown on the screen in two columns, and you can use the cursor keys to change the file name that is highlighted in some way (usually it is shown in reverse video). If there are a lot of files, you can scroll through these just as you would scroll through a Wordperfect document. All the standard methods of cursor control operate normally when using the "list files" facility (except "Go To" which is inappropriate due to the lack of pagination).

If you have some sub-directories of the Wordperfect sub-directory, you can go into these via the "list files" facility. The sub-directories are listed above the file names, and can be highlighted in exactly the same way as the file names. Use the cursor controls to highlight the required sub-directory, and press "Enter". This should result in the path to the required sub-directory being shown on the status line at the bottom of the screen. Pressing "Enter" again will take you into that sub-directory, with the files it contains being displayed on the screen. These can then be accessed in the normal way, as can any sub-directories listed in the top area of the screen.

You will notice that each file name is accompanied by three sets of figures. The first of these is the size of the file in bytes. This roughly corresponds to the number of characters in the text file, but the number of bytes used is always somewhat more than the number of characters in the file. This is due to a certain amount of space being required to store general information about the file, such as the paper size that has been selected. Also, some bytes are needed to store information about how the text is formatted. The next set of figures is simply the date when the file was created. If the file has been replaced by an updated version or versions, then this date shows the date on the last occasion that the file was updated. The third figure shows the time that the file was created or last updated. This time and date stamping is useful if you have several versions of a document on disk, and wish to ascertain which is the most up-to-date.

The very top section of the screen gives some basic information about the current document (if any), together with details of the total disk space free for use, and the amount so far used. It also shows the number of files on the disk, or in the selected sub-directory.

A number of options are listed along the bottom section of the screen. Probably the one which is needed most often is option 1, "Retrieve". This has the same effect as pressing the shift and "F10" keys, except that you are not prompted for a file name. Instead, the file that is highlighted on the screen is the one which is loaded. This is a slightly slower method of loading a file, but it has the advantage of enabling you to see what files are present on the disk. This can often be useful, as it can be difficult to remember exactly what is on a disk, especially if it contains dozens of files. Also, when supplying a file name to the computer you must get it exactly right. Even one character wrong or out of position will result in the computer reporting something like "File Not Found" and no file being loaded. Using this method removes the need to remember the exact file names you use.

Option 2 is also useful, and this is used to delete files that are no longer needed. You should not be too eager to remove files that could possibly be required at some later date. On the other hand, over a period of time it is likely that the number of files on disk will grow to the point where it is difficult to keep track of everything and that there will be no realistic likelihood of many of these files ever being needed again. If you are using a hard disk system the disk may well start to become full of files, and you will then need to go through the list of files on the disk, removing those that are of lesser importance. Even if the hard disk has plenty of spare capacity, many users prefer not to use it for the long term storage of files. Floppy disks or special tape units can be used for archive purposes and are perhaps better suited to this task than a hard disk.

To try out the "Delete" option, generate a dummy text file containing a few text characters and then try removing it using option 2. As a safety measure, pressing the "2" key does not immediately remove the file. You are asked to confirm that you wish to delete the file by pressing the "Y" key. Pressing any other key will abort the operation.

The third option is "Move/Rename", which is mainly used to rename a file (but is something you may never need to use at all). To try out this command, generate a dummy text file containing a few characters, and save it to disk under the name "text1". Then implement the "List Files" command, highlight this file name, and press "3". The left hand portion of the status line will show the name of the selected file, including the drive it is on and the path where appropriate. The file name and path can be edited using the

19

cursor keys, and changed to any valid file name, disk drive identification, and path. Apart from changing the name, you can therefore move a file from one disk to another, or from one sub-directory to another. Try moving the cursor to the end of the line, deleting "1", and replacing it with "2". If you then press "Return", the file name should change to "text2" in the list of file names. Note that the list of names is sorted into alphabetical order for you. This makes it easy to quickly locate the required file name from a long list of them. If you rename a file, it will be immediately moved, where necessary, to a new position in the list. Note that this command is slightly different in versions of Wordperfect prior to version 5.0.

Option 4 is "Print". Printing is covered in some depth in the next chapter, and this option will not be considered here. "Text In" is option 5, and this is similar to "Retrieve". However, it is for use with ASCII files. Wordperfect stores data in a fashion that is based on the standard ASCII codes, but like most word processors, it uses its own control codes for such things as indicating that a line of text should be centred. Some of these formatting commands are not available using basic ASCII codes, but something like centring a line of text is possible by using the appropriate number of space characters ahead of the text. If you wish to load in a document from another word processor, or from a text editor, this is possible provided the other word processor or text editor can save a file as a basic ASCII file. The only problem is that some characteristics of the original document may be lost in the process, due to the limitations of the basic ASCII system, or the conversion process of the word processor program.

The "Look" facility available as option 6 is a very useful one. This enables you to examine the contents of the selected file without having to load it. Any text you are currently working on is not affected by using the "Look" facility. To use this feature it is just a matter of highlighting the required file and pressing "6". As this is the default option, pressing "Return" has the same effect. The first part of the document will then be displayed on the screen, and using the cursor keys it is possible to scroll up and down through the text. You can not modify the text though. All the computer is doing is to read part of the file from disk so that its contents can be displayed on the screen. The document is not being loaded into memory in its entirety. If you are using a floppy disk system the scrolling will almost certainly be rather hesitant, and far slower than normal. With a fast hard disk system it will probably be possible to scroll through the document as quickly as normal. Press "F7" to exit from the "Look" feature.

We will not consider the other options in any detail here, but option 7 enables you to change to a different default directory, which is useful if you will be working on documents which are in a different directory, or will be creating documents that will need to be stored in a different directory. The full drive and path specification must be given when you are giving details of the new default directory. With option 8 it is possible to copy a file, either to the same disk/directory under a different name or, more realistically, to a different drive or directory. Option 9 is the "Word Search" facility. This enables files to be searched for a particular word or character pattern. An "*" is marked against any files which contain the specified word or character pattern.

Bold, Underline, Etc.

Most printers support bold type, which is usually produced by printing the text twice. Underlining is also supported by the vast majority of printers and both of these features are available via Wordperfect. They are selected using "F6" and "F8" respectively. These keys provide a toggle action — press them once to switch on bold/underlining — press them again to switch it off. You do not have to select one or the other, and it is perfectly alright to use both at once if necessary. With most screens the bold text will not appear in bold type on the screen, and underlined text may not be shown complete with the underlining. Inverse video or colour changes are usually used to indicate the changes in text style.

If your system has a colour monitor you can select the colours used for bold, underlined, and bold and underlined text, as well as the colours used for other special types of text. First the initial setup screen must be accessed by pressing the shift key and "F1". This gives access to a great many parameters, and it is well worthwhile studying this screen for a while to see what options are available to you. The option you require is number 3 ("Display"), and from the new menu screen this produces you require option 2 ("Colours/Fonts/Attributes"). This takes you into another menu screen, from which you should select option 1 ("Screen Colours"). The screen should then show the available text types, whether they appear underlined or not, their current foreground and background colours, and an example of what each type of text actually looks

Setup: Colours/Fonts　　　　　A B C D E F G H
　　　　　　　　　　　　　　　A B C D E F G H

Attribute	Font	Foreground	Background	Sample
Normal	N	C	A	Sample
Blocked	N	B	H	Sample
Underline	Y	H	A	Sample
Strikeout	N	C	B	Sample
Bold	N	B	A	Sample
Double Underline	N	F	B	Sample
Redline	N	E	B	Sample
Shadow	N	A	D	Sample
Italics	N	B	D	Sample
Small Caps	N	E	D	Sample
Outline	N	F	D	Sample
Subscript	N	G	D	Sample
Superscript	N	H	D	Sample
Fine Print	N	B	A	Sample
Small Print	N	C	A	Sample
Large Print	N	D	A	Sample
Very Large Print	N	A	C	Sample
Extra Large Print	N	F	A	Sample
Bold & Underline	Y	E	A	Sample
Other Combinations	N	A	G	Sample

Switch to switch; Move to copy settings　　　Doc 1

Fig.1.2　The screen colours menu. This may vary slightly from one display type to another.

like (as in Figure 1.2). At the top of the screen a little colour chart will appear, showing which colour each code letter represents, when the cursor is in one of the colour selection columns. You simply type in the letters for the colours you want for each type of text. Also, if you require the text to be underlined, you place a "Y" in the underline column. Two presses of "F7" will take you out of the colours setup screen and back to the main screen.

It is often necessary to have headings centred, and this can be achieved by pressing the shift key and "F6" prior to typing in the heading. The centring only operates on a line by line basis. If you wish to have several lines centred, then you must press the shift key and "F6" at the beginning of each one. As an alternative to implementing the "Centre" command and then typing in the line of text, you can type in the line of text, set the cursor to the beginning of the line to be centred, and then press the shift key and "F6". This is useful if you are editing a document and decide to centre a few lines.

Reveal Codes

There is a slight problem if you wish to undertake tasks such as uncentring a line, or changing bold text to normal text. Features such as bold and centred text are implemented by having control characters embedded in the text. These control characters can be removed using the delete and backspace keys if you change your mind about something, but they can be difficult to locate as they are not displayed on the screen. Normally only their effect is visible.

This problem can easily be overcome by using the "Reveal Codes" command. This command is implemented by pressing "Alt" and "F3". If your computer is equipped with a 101/102 key IBM style keyboard, pressing "F11" will have the same effect (provided the hardware and software properly supports 101 and 102 key keyboards). When you press "F11" the screen is split into two "windows". In the upper one the text is displayed normally, but in the lower window the control characters are shown. To be more accurate about it, brief descriptions of the codes enclosed in square brackets are shown in the lower window. This makes it easy to delete any unwanted control codes. Simply move the cursor onto the unwanted code (which will result in the control code characters being highlighted), and press the delete key. In order to revert to normal operation you merely need to press "Alt" and "F3" again (or "F11" if you have a suitable keyboard). Incidentally, the undelete facility might not give the desired effect if used with control codes.

Tabs

The "Tab" (tabulation) key is on the extreme left hand side of the main keyboard area on most keyboards. It is often marked with a couple of arrows, one pointing left and one pointing right, rather than being marked "Tab". Its purpose is to move the cursor to preset positions across the screen. If you try pressing this key a few times, you will find that each time it is pressed the cursor jumps five character positions to the right. This is the default setting of Wordperfect, but you can set the tab positions wherever you like.

Suppose that you wish to have new paragraphs indented by ten character positions. You could simply press the "Tab" key twice at the beginning of each paragraph, or you could change the default tab positions to give the required ten character indentation with a single key press. In order to set the tab positions you must first invoke the "Format" command by pressing "Shift" and "F8". Then select option 1 ("Line") followed by option 8 ("Tab Set"). You will then see the tabulation ruler at the bottom of the screen, with "L" characters used to mark the positions of the default tabulation points at five character intervals. The cursor can be moved along the ruler using the left and right cursor keys. Unwanted tabs can be removed by placing the cursor under the appropriate "L" character, and then pressing the "delete" key. New tab stops can be added by placing the cursor at the appropriate position on the ruler and typing in the apposite character.

There are four characters to choose from, and each one gives different formatting of the text which follows the tab character. An "L" character gives left justified text, and is the normal tab character. An "R" gives right justified text, which means that the text "grows" to the left of the tab stop, rather than progressing over to the left in the normal way. A "C" character gives text that is centred about the tab stop position. Finally, a "D" gives right justification until the "tab align" character (a full stop by default) is typed. The text then "grows" to the right of the tab stop position in the usual manner.

In our example it is merely necessary to place the cursor under the first tab stop, and to press "delete" in order to remove it. The required tab stop at character position ten is already present. Suppose that a complex table had to be produced, and that tab stops were required at character positions 12, 19, 28, 43, 57, and 62. Since none of the existing tab stops are at these positions the first job would be to clear all the existing tab stops using the "delete" key and the cursor keys. You would then have to move the cursor to the appropriate positions, typing a "L", "R", "C", or "D" at each one. If tab stops are required at regular intervals, there is a quick way of setting them. Simply type in the position of the first tab stop, followed by the required distance between subsequent tab stops.

Remember that the tab rulers operate in terms of inches, not character positions. Much printing is done at ten characters to the inch, and so it is not too difficult to convert tab ruler measures into character positions if that is the type of measure you would rather work in. Also remember that there are left and right hand margins, which (if left at their default values) are each one inch wide. Consequently, if you required the first tab stop fifteen characters (1.5 inches) in from the left margin, and the tabs spaced ten characters (1 inch) apart thereafter, the first tab stop would be at 2.5 inches and not 1.5 inches. You would therefore type in "2.5,1".

Many newcomers to Wordperfect get into difficulties with the formatting commands as they fail to realise that they do not necessarily set the format for the entire document. They will control the format of the whole document if they are used before you start typing the document, and they are not changed at any later point in the document. However, you can change the tab positions and many other aspects of the document's format as often as you wish, simply by issuing new format commands at various points in the document. This sort of control is absent from many word processors, and is a very powerful feature of Wordperfect. If you should need to use a lot of formatting commands in a document, remember that the "Reveal Codes" command can be used to show exactly what formatting codes are present in the document, should things not be quite as expected.

We have by no means covered the full range of formatting commands here, but we will not consider any more of them in this chapter. Topics such as page numbering, justification, and line spacing are covered in the next chapter, which deals with printing out documents.

Search
When word processing you might occasionally find that a word or

phrase you have been using is incorrect in some way. Going through the document to manually locate and change every occurrence of the offending word or phrase could take a very long time. The ability to automatically search for a specified text string, and optionally replace it with a different set of characters, is a basic word processing function. As one would expect of a high performance word processor such as Wordperfect, it has excellent search and replace capbilities.

In order to use the search facility it must first be accessed by pressing "F2". This brings up the message "—> Srch:" on the status line. You then type in the string of text that must be searched for, and this can include any printable characters plus carriage returns, spaces, and tab stops. In order to invoke the search the "F2" key is pressed again. If the text string is not found, the status line will show the message "Not Found". If the text string is present in the document, the program will move to the page where it first occurs, and place the cursor one character position beyond the end of the string. If you wish to search for the same text string further down in the document, simply press "F2" twice in order to initiate a new search.

An important point to bear in mind is that the search command only searches text that is after the cursor position when the search command is instigated. If the cursor is at the end of the document, the search command has no effect, and will always return the "Not Found" message. In order to search the entire document you must ensure that the cursor is taken to the very beginning of the document before calling up the search function. There is an alternative "Search" command which is obtained by pressing "Shift" and "F2", rather than simply pressing "F2". This operates in exactly the same way as the other "Search" command, but it searches backwards from the current cursor position.

A certain amount of care needs to be exercised when deciding on the search string to enter, as it is all too easy to enter a string which crops up unexpectedly. For instance, the string "sting" would be located in the word "interesting", "string", and probably in many other words as well. Where the string you are searching for is a whole word, Wordperfect can be prevented from picking out that string from within larger words by using a space before and after the word. Note that lower case letters will match with both upper and lower case letters. However, if you enter upper case letters, these will only match with upper case letters.

There is an extended search facility which is invoked by pressing "Home" prior to pressing "F2'. When you have typed in the search string, it is then only necessary to press "F2" (not "Home" and then ' F2"). The extended search differs from the standard version of the command in that it also searches through headers, footers, endnotes, etc., as well as the main body of text.

Search and Replace

The search and replace function (just called "Replace" in Word-perfect terminology) is obtained by pressing the "Alt" and "F2" keys. This will bring up the message "w/Confirm? (Y/N)" on the status line. This is asking you whether or not you wish to confirm each replacement, or you want the computer to go through the document automatically implementing each replacement with no manual intervention. Unless you are reasonably sure that the computer will only turn up instances of the text string that you will wish to be changed, it is obviously much safer to opt for manual confirmation by typing "Y". If a lot of changes will be needed, the process will obviously be much quicker and easier if you simply let the computer get on with it by typing "N".

Once you have typed "Y" or "N", the status line gives the same message that appears for the search command. You then type in the appropriate search string, and this operates using the same rules that apply for the search function. When the correct search string has been typed in, press "F2" to bring up the message "Replace with:", and type in the new string of characters. If you used a space at each end of the string in the search pattern, then you should do the same when typing in the replacement text string. Otherwise the spaces between the replacement text and the words either side of it will be eliminated.

Double Documents

As pointed out previously, Wordperfect has the ability to operate with two documents in memory at once. You can only work on one or the other at any one time of course, and you switch between the two by pressing the "Shift" and "F3" keys. If you try this you will notice that the right portion of the status line will change from "Doc 1 . . . ." to "Doc 2 . . . .". You may also find that the screen colours change, since each document has its own format, with different screen colours, line space, etc., if desired. It is a good idea to set up the two documents to have totally different colour schemes as you can then see at a glance which one you are working on. To switch back to document 1 simply press "Shift" and "F3" again.

As an alternative to having each document with its own screen, you can split the screen so that both documents can be viewed at once, each with its own status line. This feature is accessed via the "Screen" command, which is invoked by pressing "Ctrl" and "F3". Select option 1 ("Window"), and then type in the number of screen lines you want the current document to occupy. To split the screen into two (more or less) equal parts a value of twelve is normally required. However, this obviously depends on the type of display you are using, and in some cases it is possible to have more than twenty lines per window.

Even with the screen split into two windows, obviously you can still only work on one document at a time. You switch from one document to the other using "Shift" and "F3", as before. This switches the cursor from one window to the other. Also, with the split screen operation a tab ruler appears between the windows, and the arrow heads which mark the tab positions point to whichever window is active. In order to switch back to single window operation, invoke the "Display" command again, and again select the "Window" option. Give the number of lines as twenty-four, or whatever number of lines your type of display uses, and press return. You should then be in the current document with single window operation.

Margins
Wordperfect can handle a wide range of paper sizes, and gives you complete control over the width of top, bottom, left, and right hand margin sizes. To select the required paper size use the "Format" command by pressing "Shift" and "F8". Then select option 2 ("Page"), followed by option 8 ("Paper Size/Type"). This brings up a list of various 'A' and U.S. paper sizes, and you simply choose the one you will be using. If you are going to use an unusual or non-standard paper size, you can select option "U" ("User Defined"), and then enter the width and height of the paper.

The top and bottom margin sizes are also accessed using the "Format" command and the "Page" option. However, you then select option 5, "Margins — Top/Bottom". When you press key "5" you will notice that the cursor moves to the top margin measurement. Type in the new size (there is no need to include the inches (") character after the top margin measurement) and press "Return". This moves the cursor down to the bottom margin measurement, where you again type in the new figure and press return.

The left and right hand margins are controlled via the "Format" command, but they are set using the "Line" option (option 1), followed by option 7 ("Margins — Left/Right"). This operates in exactly the same way as the top and bottom margin settings. In order to exit from either command once you have put in the new settings, simply press "F7" once. Remember that these formatting commands can be inserted into a document as and where necessary. You do not need to use the same margin settings for every page. If you do want the margin settings to affect every page, the format commands must be issued at the very beginning of the document. You do not have to issue them before starting to type anything — it is quite alright to add them ahead of existing text.

You can only set up large page sizes if they are supported by your printer, and that printer is installed as the current one. We will not go into the subject of printers here, as this is an important topic which has its own chapter. Before using Wordperfect in earnest you should install the correct printer driver or drivers, and set up the printer format correctly, as you could otherwise run into difficulties later.

If you do use a large page size, or a small print size, you will have a document which prints with a maximum line length of more than 80 characters. Some displays can handle up to about 132 column text, but most have a maximum of 80 characters per line. This does not mean that with an 80 column display you can not produce documents that will print out at more than 80 characters to the line. Wordperfect can handle massive pages with any type of display. It does so using a system of scrolling, similar to the vertical scrolling used to enable long documents to be accommodated. In addition to this method of scrolling, horizontal scrolling is used to accommodate long lines. Like the vertical variety, with horizontal scrolling the screen automatically scrolls to keep the cursor within the screen area when you are adding text. The cursor control methods all work normally, but there are a couple of extra methods of cursor control available when horizontal scrolling is in operation. If you press "Home" twice before operating the left or right cursor keys, the cursor moves right to the beginning or end of the current line. A single press on "Home" prior to operating the left or right cursor keys takes the cursor fully left or right on the screen, not necessarily to the beginning or end of the line.

Auto Repeat
The auto repeat that operates on virtually all the keys of the keyboard was mentioned previously, but there is an alternative automatic repeat facility available in Wordperfect. This repeats the specified character a preset number of times. To obtain this form of auto repeat you must first press the "Escape" key. This produces the message "Repeat Value = 8" on the status line. If the default value of eight is not the required number of repetitions, you must first type in the number of repetitions that are required. Then press the key for the character that you wish to be repeated, and it will be produced the specified number of times. If you want to change the default to a value other than 8, press "Escape", type in the new default value, and then press "Return".

There seems to be a slight flaw in this method of auto repeating characters in that if you press "Escape" and then operate one of the number keys, Wordperfect will assume that you are typing in the number of repetitions you require, not the character you want repeated. Consequently, it would seem to be impossible to use this feature to auto repeat the number characters.

Text In/Out
The "Text In" feature has been covered previously, but only as one of the options of the "List Files" command. There is in fact a more comprehensive version of the command available as the "Text In/Out" feature, accessed by pressing "Ctrl" and "F5". This brings up a list of options on the status line, but for basic ASCII saving and loading you must press either "1" or "T" to select the "DOS Text" option. This brings a list of three further options on the status line, one of which is to save the current document as a DOS compatible ASCII file (option 1, "Save;"). The other two options are slightly different forms of "Retrieve", and they differ in the way in which they handle hard return characters. The best way to find out which one handles your ASCII documents the best is to try them both to see. In some cases it will probably not make very much difference.

When retrieving DOS text files you may find that neither version of the "Retrieve" command gives a properly formatted document on the screen. This could be due to the source not being a true DOS

ASCII file, but some form of word processor file which includes control codes that are having an adverse effect on the formatting. You can even end up with unusual characters on the screen (which are text and graphics characters from the extended IBM character set) where control codes have been interpreted as printable characters. There is no easy solution to this problem. If you go back to the program which produced the troublesome file you might find a way of saving the file as a true ASCII type. Alternatively, it might be possible to obtain a document conversion program that will convert the source file into Wordperfect 5.0 format, or some other format that Wordperfect can handle properly.

If the problem is simply that what should be single lines of text are spread over two lines, or something of this type, it can usually be solved by increasing or decreasing the maximum line length Wordperfect is set up to handle. A little experimentation is called for here, but many DOS text files are set for a maximum line length of 80 characters, and for satisfactory results you will often need to set Wordperfect for this line length, or an even longer one.

Option 3 of the "Text In/Out" command ("Save Generic;") saves the document in a form that has any Wordperfect control codes filtered out, but which, as far as possible, maintains the format of the document. Where a line is centred for instance, spaces are used ahead of the text in order to provide centring. This might give better results than saving a document as a DOS text file when exporting documents to other programs. It is certainly worth trying if the DOS text file output gives less than entirely satisfactory results.

Documents can be saved in Wordperfect 4.2 format by using option 4 ("Save WP 4.2;"). This could be necessary if you wish to send disk files to someone who is running version 4.2 of Wordperfect. Also, you might have a program such as a grammar checker that can not handle Wordperfect 5.0 format files, but which will work perfectly well with version 4.2 files.

There are two further options available under the "Text In/Out" command, one of which is the "Password" option (option 2). This enables so-called "locked" documents to be produced. These are documents saved on disk files which can not be loaded into or printed from Wordperfect without first giving the correct password. When you select option 2 you are given two further options on the status line, the first of which is "Add/Change;". If you select this option, you will be prompted for the new password, which can be up to twenty-four characters long. The password does not appear on the screen as you type it. This is a common computer security measure, and it ensures that someone behind you can not easily see what password you have selected. It means that you will not be able to see if you have made a typing error, and consequently the program requires you to type in the password twice. The password is only accepted if what you type in is exactly the same both times. If you make a mistake either time you must start again from the beginning. The other option available under the password command is "Remove", which simply removes any existing password from the document so that it is no longer in locked format, and can be retrieved normally.

The password facility is obviously a great asset if there are several people using the same computer, and you wish to ensure that no one can read or tamper with your files. On the other hand, if you should happen to forget a password you will be locked out of your own files, probably with no realistic chance of ever being able to read them again! The document files produced using the password feature of Wordperfect are heavily encrypted, and can not be read using a disk editor. At least, the characters stored on the disk will be readable, but will be scrambled and meaningless. This feature is a good one for those who need it and use it carefully, but it is not one that you should use otherwise.

Comments

Although accessed via the "Text In/Out" command, comments are not strictly speaking anything to do with the loading or saving of text. A comment in this context is some text which can be displayed on the screen or hidden, as required, but which is not printed out on the final document. However, comments can be converted into normal text that will be printed out if desired.

The comment facility is accessed by selecting option 5 ("Comment:") from the "Text In/Out" menu. The status line then offers three choices, the first of which is to create a comment. If you press "1" to select this option, you will be presented with an on-screen box into which your comment can be typed. Bold, underline, and all Wordperfect characters are available when typing a comment. Once you have finished, press "F7" to exit back to the main text screen. The comment box will be displayed on the screen, and will obviously have altered to some degree the format of the text on the screen. It has no affect on the printed out document though.

Option 2 enables an existing comment to be edited. The comment that is made available for editing is the one which the program finds when looking backwards from the current cursor position. Therefore, you must position the cursor just after the comment that you wish to edit. The third option converts a comment to ordinary text which will be printed out with the rest of the document. Again, you must position the cursor just after the comment that you wish to process before issuing this command. Only the text in the comment box will be shown on the screen after conversion. The comment box itself is removed.

If you wish to remove a comment from a document there are two options. The first one genuinely removes the comment, and involves changing the comment to ordinary text and then deleting it in the usual way. The second method is to switch off comments so that they are not displayed on the screen. They are still present in the document though, and can be switched back on again should you wish to do so. This method only permits all comments to be switched on or off — you can not selectively enable and disable each comment box. Whether or not comments are displayed is controlled by the "Setup" command, which is accessed by pressing "Shift" and "F1". Option 3 ("Display") must be selected, and on the menu screen that this produces (Figure 1.3) select option 3 again and type in "Y" or "N" (for yes or no) as appropriate. Press "F7" to exit back to the document screen. Note that if comments are made "invisible" by this means, their presence can still be shown using the "Reveal Codes" command.

It is possible to convert ordinary text into a comment by first defining a block of text, then pressing "Ctrl" and "F5" to invoke the "Text In/Out" command, then answering "Y" in answer to the prompt on the status line. The method used to define a block of text is covered in the next section of this chapter.

Block Operations
It is often much quicker and easier to perform a word processor function that must operate on a medium to large chunk of text if the block of text can be grouped together as a single entity and processed en masse, rather than having to change things on a character by character basis. Perhaps the most obvious example of this is when deleting a large section of text. It can take a long time to digest a large chunk of text using the delete keys. It is much easier

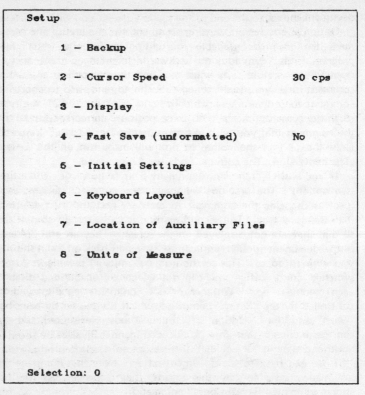

```
Setup

    1 - Backup

    2 - Cursor Speed                    30 cps

    3 - Display

    4 - Fast Save (unformatted)          No

    5 - Initial Settings

    6 - Keyboard Layout

    7 - Location of Auxiliary Files

    8 - Units of Measure




Selection: 0
```

Fig.1.3 The setup menu. This gives access to further menus.

to indicate the start point for the deletion, use the cursor control
keys to move the cursor to the end point and mark it, and then
delete the marked text in one go.

This function is available using Wordperfect's "Block" command.
Try entering some text for test purposes, move the cursor to the
start of the section you have selected for deletion, and press "Alt"
plus "F4" to start the "Block" command. If your computer is
equipped with an IBM 101/102 keyboard, pressing "F12" is an
alternative method of invoking the "Block" command. Once the
"Block" command has been initiated, a "Block On" message will
flash on and off at the left hand section of the status line. You then

move the cursor to the end of the section of text you wish to delete. In actual fact it is quite acceptable to start at the end of the block and then move upwards to the starting point. Either way the block will be defined properly, and will be highlighted on the screen so that you can see exactly what text will be affected by any block command. If you should change your mind, and wish to abort the block operation, simply press "Alt" and "F4" (or "F12") again to turn the block command off. Once you have correctly selected the block of text for deletion, simply operate the "Delete" key, and answer "Y" in response to the prompt on the status line ("Delete Block? Y/N).

The "Block" command can be used in conjunction with other commands, such as converting text into a comment, as described previously. It can also be used to print a selected portion of text, and this is covered in the next chapter. One of the main uses of the block command is in conjunction with the "Copy" and "Move" commands. As pointed out previously, the delete and undelete functions can be used as a means of copying and moving text, but Wordperfect provides commands specifically for these functions.

If we start with block moves, the first task is to define the section of text to be moved, and this is done in exactly the same manner as when selecting a block of text for deletion. Having selected the correct section of text, the "Move" command is invoked by pressing "Ctrl" and "F4". Next the "Block" option is selected by pressing the "1" key, and then the "Move" option is selected by pressing the "1" key again. You then move the cursor to the new position for the text and press "Return", as directed by the prompt on the status line.

The block copy command operates in much the same way, with the block of text first being defined, then "Ctrl" and "F4" being operated in order to invoke the "Move" command, and then key "1" being pressed in order to select the "Block" option. However, you then select the "Copy" option by pressing key "2", before repositioning the cursor and pressing "Return" in order to place the copied text in the desired position.

Another form of block operation is case conversion. Suppose you accidentally leave the "Caps Lock" key in the on position, and type in a lot of text before you realise that it is mainly in upper case text (capital letters) when it should in fact be mainly in lower case (small) letters. You could simply delete the offending text and then retype it, but the block case conversion offers a more simple alternative. First you must define the block of text to be converted using the "Block" command in the usual manner. Next press "Shift" and "F3" to invoke the "Switch" command. Two options will then be shown on the status line, which are "1 Uppercase;" and "2 Lowercase;". Type "1" or "U" to convert all the text in the block to upper case. Type "2" or "L" in order to convert all the text in the block to lower case lettering. Note that you can only set the entire block to upper case or the entire block to lower case. There is no option which permits the case of all letters to be swopped.

Widows and Orphans

With Wordperfect there is no need for you to put in page breaks. You set up the program to use a particular size of paper, with margins of a certain size, and it puts in page breaks automatically for you every "X" number of lines. This basic method has its limitations, and you can sometimes find a heading at the bottom of the page with the text for that heading on the following page or pages, or perhaps the first line of a paragraph at the bottom of the page with the rest of the paragraph on the next page. This is termed an "orphan".

There is an allied problem where the final page has just one line of text, or perhaps even just one word. Similarly, the last line of a paragraph could be left off the same page as the rest of the paragraph, and placed on the next page. This is termed a "widow".

Wordperfect provides more than one way of avoiding this type of thing. One method is the "Block Protect" feature which can be used to ensure that a paragraph is not split up by a soft page break. To use the "Block Protect" command you first use the "Block" command to highlight the text that must be protected, in the standard fashion. Then press "Shift" and "F8", followed by "Y" in answer to the prompt "Protect block? (Y/N)".

An alternative method is to use the "Conditional End Of Page" feature, which protects a specified number of lines from being split by a page break. This is different to the "Block Protect" feature in that it covers a fixed number of lines. With the "Block Protect" feature a "Block Protect On" control code is placed at the beginning of the block, and a "Block Protect Off" control code is placed at the end. If the block has text deleted or added, the size of the block is effectively altered in order to suit the new size of the paragraph.

The "Conditional End Of Page" facility is accessed via the "Format" command ("Shift" and "F8"). Then select option 4 ("Other") followed by option 2 ("Conditional End Of Page"). You will then be prompted on the status line to indicate the number of lines to be kept together. Type in the appropriate number followed by "Return" and then press "F7" to exit from the command and return to the main document screen.

For most purposes the "Widows and Orphans" feature is adequate. Unlike the other two methods, it only prevents single lines appearing at the top/bottom of a page, but this is normally all that is required. It has the advantage of operating fully automatically without any intervention by the user. To switch on this feature, first invoke the "Format" command by pressing "Shift" and "F8". Then select option 1 ("Line") followed by option 9 ("Widow/ Orphan Protection"). Type "Y" to turn on widow and orphan protection, or "N" to switch it off. Press "F7" to exit this command and return to the document screen. Like many of Wordperfect's formatting commands, the widows and orphans facility can be switched on and off at various points in the document, as required. In order to set widow/orphan protection for the entire document, switch on this facility with the cursor right at the very beginning of the document.

The page breaks inserted automatically are termed "soft" page breaks. You can insert page breaks manually, and these are called "hard" page breaks. There is not normally any need for hard page breaks to be added, but suppose you put a table into the middle of a document, and you want that table to be on a page of its own. This can be achieved by preceding it with a hard page break, and putting another one immediately after it. This assumes that the table will fit onto one page. Obviously if it is very long it will be spread over two or more pages by Wordperfect's automatic "soft" page insertion process.

In order to insert a hard page break in a document you simply press "Ctrl" and "Return". This places a line of equals ("=") signs across the screen to indicate the position of the hard page break. Soft page breaks incidentally, are shown by a series of minus signs ("−") across the screen. A hard page break can be removed using the "Reveal" Codes" command to show up the control code so that it can be deleted. Alternatively, simply position the cursor at the beginning of the line of equals signs and press "Delete".

Twin Columns

For applications such as typing a newsletter, more professional results can be obtained by using two columns of text. This feature is available to Wordperfect users under the "Math/Columns" command. To invoke this command press "Alt" and "F7". However, note that before you can switch the columns feature on, you must define the columns. The columns definition procedure starts by invoking the "Math/Columns" command ("Alt" plus "F7"). Then select option 4, "Columns Def:" to bring up the columns definition menu page (Figure 1.4). There is a choice of three column styles, which are newspaper (option 1), parallel (option 2), or parallel with block protect on (option 3). Newspaper columns are the usual type, where the text runs down to the end of one column, then carries on from the top of the next column, and so on. Parallel columns are used where you want a small amount of text in the first column, then some more text in the next column, further text in the next one, and so on. In other words, it is used for such things as lists and inventories.

If you are happy with the default column positions and widths, press "F7" to return to the main "Math/Columns" menu, and then press "3" to switch on the columns feature. This switches on the twin columns, and also takes you back to the main document screen.

For many purposes the default settings will suffice, but you can easily design your own columns if you wish. You are not even limited to twin columns, and it is possible to have up to twenty-four columns. However, being practical about it, a large page width is needed in order to use more than about four or five columns. To define your own columns, first select option 2 ("Number Of Columns") and type in the number of columns you require followed by "Return". Using option 3 ("Distance Between Columns") you then specify the distance between the columns, and again press "Return". The bottom part of the screen will then show just where each column appears on the page. These default settings will normally be perfectly satisfactory, but if desired you can select option 4 ("Margins") and alter the settings to precisely match your requirements.

When you type text into newspaper style columns, the text flows down column 1 until the end of the page is reached. Wordperfect then adds a soft page break, but it then goes to the top of column 2 instead of going on to the next page. When the end of the

```
Text Column Definition

1 — Type                                      News paper

2 — Number of Columns                         5

3 — Distance Between Columns                  0.36"

4 — Margins

Column   Left     Right       Column
1:       1"       2.02"       13:
2:       2.37"    3.39"       14:
3:       3.74"    4.76"       15:
4:       5.11"    6.13"       16:
5:       6.48"    7.5"        17:
6:                            18:
7:                            19:
8:                            20:
9:                            21:
10:                           22:
11:                           23:
12:                           24:

Selection: 0
```

Left   Right

Fig.1.4 The column definition menu

39

last column is reached, a soft page break is added, but this time the following text is placed at the top of column 1 in the next page. Automatic pagination is therefore provided when Wordperfect is in the columns mode of operation.

In most respects there is no difference in the way in which Wordperfect is used when it is used with two or more columns. It necessitates some minor changes in the way that the cursor control operates, together with some effect on commands such as the "Move" one. You can not use comments or footnotes, or adjust the columns definition and margins when working within columns. It might be more convenient to have the text displayed in a single column while typing in text or editing the document. This will increase the speed with which the screen will scroll and be re-written, and is probably much easier to work with as well. In order to switch to a single column display press "Shift" and "F1" to bring up the main "Setup" display. Then select option 3 ("Display") followed by option 8 ("Side-By-Side Columns Display"). Type "N" to go into single column display mode, or "Y" if you are in the single column mode and wish to switch back to side-by-side operation.

DOS Commands

When you are using Wordperfect it can be necessary to perform an operating system command. Suppose, for example, that you wish to save a document to a new sub-directory, but you have forgotten to create the new sub-directory before running Wordperfect. You could get around this problem by saving the program in the Wordperfect sub-directory on a temporary basis, creating the new sub-directory when you have exited Wordperfect, copying the file to the new sub-directory, and then deleting the original version of the file. This is a bit long-winded though, and it would be much easier if you could create the new sub-directory from within Wordperfect, and then save the document direct to that sub-directory.

It is possible to perform DOS commands using Wordperfect's "Shell" command. Suppose that we wish to create a sub-directory called "book1", which must be a sub-directory of the Wordperfect sub-directory. First the "Shell" command must be invoked by pressing "Ctrl" and "F1". Press the "1" key to select option 1, which is the only option apart from option 0 which aborts the "Shell" command. You should now see an ordinary DOS screen, except it will contain the message "Enter 'EXIT' to return to

Wordperfect". Note that this does not mean that you press the "Exit" function key ("F7") in order to return to Wordperfect. You must actually type the word "exit" and then press the "Return" key, and it does not matter whether the letters are in upper or lower case (or a mixture of the two). In effect, "exit" is a new DOS command which takes you back into Wordperfect. Once you have returned to Wordperfect, everything should be just as you left it.

In our example we wish to create a new sub-directory. This is achieved using the "mkdir" command (which can be abbreviated to just "md"). Therefore, typing "md book1" and pressing "Return" will create the new directory. Typing "exit" followed by pressing "Return" will take you back into Wordperfect again. The current document can then be saved to the new directory in the normal manner. Note that if you wish to use an external DOS command such as "format", it is quite acceptable to change to the DOS sub-directory, use the external command or commands, and then return to Wordperfect in the normal way. You do not need to be in the Wordperfect sub-directory before you type "exit" and return to the program. The "exit" command seems to operate perfectly well from any sub-directory or the root directory.

Date

IBM PCs (and many other computers) have a built in clock/calendar function. Wordperfect can access this so that it can place the date in documents. Obviously the computer's clock/calendar must be correctly set up if Wordperfect's date facility is to operate properly. The method of setting up the clock depends on the type of computer you are using, but with IBM PC/ATs and compatibles the "Setup" program is used to set the clock.

In order to use the "Date" command press "Shift" and "F5" to bring up the date and outline options on the status lines. There are then three date options available to you (options "1" to "3"). Option 1 ("Date Text;") places the date at the current cursor position as a piece of straightforward text (e.g. "11 May 1989"), which will always be displayed on screen and printed out the same. Pressing the "2" key to select option 2 ("Date Code;") appears to have exactly the same effect, but the date is actually inserted in the document as a control code rather than text. The difference this makes is that if you reload the document or print it out at some later date, the correct date will be displayed and printed. If you are keeping copies of letters on disk in case you need to refer back

```
Date Format

Character    Meaning

1            Day of the Month
2            Month (number)
3            Month (word)
4            Year (all four digits)
5            Year (last two digits)
6            Day of the Week (word)
7            Hour (24-hour clock)
8            Hour (12-hour clock)
9            Minute
0            am / pm
%            Used before a number, will:
             Pad numbers less than 10 with a leading zero
             Output only 3 letters for the month or day of the week

Examples:    3 1, 4       = December 25, 1984
             %6 %3 1, 4   = Tue Dec 25, 1984
             %2/%1/5 (6)  = 01/01/85 (Tuesday)
             8:90         = 10:55am

Date format: 1 3 4
```

Fig.1.5 The date format menu gives tremendous control over the way the date/time is automatically printed.

42

to them, it is option 1 that you should choose, so that you can see the date each letter was sent. If you are making up some standard letters, use option 2 so that the correct date is automatically put into each standard letter you send.

The third option ("Date Format;") enables you to select the required format for the date. This brings up a menu screen (Figure 1.5) which is largely self-explanatory. You choose the particular pieces of date/time you want, and type the appropriate numbers. If you require spaces between each section of the date, then use spaces between the selection numbers. In fact you can use any characters you like between each part of the date, but bear in mind that you must not exceed a total of 29 characters. You should have little difficulty in setting up the date facility to provide virtually any required date/time format.

Finally
This covers all you need to know in order to enter text into Wordperfect efficiently, and to edit it. It also covers some aspects of formatting text to suit your requirements. More information on getting the format correct is provided in the next chapter, which deals with getting your documents printed out. The only way of learning to use a complex program such as Wordperfect is to try it out in practice, but it is a good idea to play around with the program a little before starting to use it in earnest. Try out as many of the commands as possible, making note of any that seem likely to be of use to you when you start working with the program properly. Try to keep in mind any facilities for which you have no immediate use. You might encounter a problem later on which can be solved with the aid of such a command. Initially though, concentrate on the features you are likely to use a lot, and try to get to the stage where you can use them intuitively.

Before using the program in earnest you should read through the next chapter and get the program set up to operate with your printer or printers. It is not absolutely essential to get the printer installation process completed before you start entering documents into the system, but it does avoid possible complications later on.

Chapter 2

PRINTING OUT

I suppose that a printer is not an essential part of word processing. You might wish to use a word processor for producing text files containing program listings for a compiler or interpreter, it might be needed to produce personal notes which you can read off the screen and do not need as hard copy, or you might only need to send documents to other parties in the form of files on floppy disks. Being realistic about it though, probably more than 99% of word processor users need to regularly print out documents. Wordperfect 5.0 is well equipped to format pages in the required way, and it can be used effectively with a wide range of printers. If there is no driver specifically for your printer, then it is quite likely that one of the supplied printer drivers will still suffice. Most new printers are designed to be compatible with a well known printer or range of printers, so that they are usable with a wide range of existing software. As a few examples, many nine pin dot matrix printers are compatible with the Epson FX range, many twenty-four pin types are compatible with the Epson LQ range, and many laser (or similar page type printers) are compatible with the HP Laserjet Plus. If you can not find a Wordperfect driver for your particular printer, study its manual to see if it offers an emulation of a printer that is supported by Wordperfect.

Printers
Before you can print out anything from Wordperfect it must have at least one printer installed. In this context "installed" does not mean simply connecting the printer to the computer via the appropriate port. It also means telling Wordperfect which printer you are using so that it can select the correct driver for that printer. The driver is data on one of the disks supplied as part of the Wordperfect package, which is used by the part of the program that sends data to the printer. This might seem to be unnecessary, since virtually all printers use standard ASCII codes to select the characters that will be printed out. However, in practice things are not quite as simple as this.

Wordperfect enables quite flexible formatting of text, with features such as bold text, underlined text, condensed or large lettering, various pitches (various numbers of characters to the inch), and even graphics can be included in documents (but not in versions prior to 5.0). ASCII codes may be standardised, but there are various methods of coding for such things as changing fonts, printing graphics, etc. Page printers often work using quite sophisticated page description languages, and need to be fed with more than a simple string of ASCII characters.

Wordperfect must be set up to do things in a way that is compatible with your printer. It is important to realise that not all the facilities of Wordperfect are available with all printers. Obviously a printer with graphics capability is needed if you intend to incorporate graphics in your documents. Most printers can handle graphics these days, but results are much better with some than with others, and being realistic about it, daisywheel printers have to be regarded as text only devices. Features such as italics and reduced or enlarged lettering are not available on all printers. The manual for your printer should give a good idea of what can and can not be achieved, but it might be necessary to adopt a "suck-it-and-see" approach in order to ascertain exactly what formatting features are available to you.

Of course, if you only produce simple documents which do not use any special formatting features, or only utilize some of the more basic ones such as centring of headings, bold text, and underlined text, then virtually any standard ASCII printer should be able to handle the job.

Installation

The procedure for installing a printer driver is to start by invoking the "Print"command. To do this press "Shift" and "F7", which will bring up the initial print screen. This offers a number of options (Figure 2.1), but in this case it is "Select Printer" (press the "S" key) under the options heading that is required. This brings a list of installed printers at the top of the screen, but only if at least one printer has been installed. The status line shows further options, and if you are installing a new printer it is option 2 ("Additional Printers") that is required. Wordperfect will provide a message along the lines "Printer Files Not Found" unless it can find some printer drivers in the correct disk drive. This is drive A for a hard disk system, or drive B for a twin floppy disk system. Alternatively, you might get a range of further options on the status line, one of which is to specify the disk drive in which the

```
Print

        1 — Full Document
        2 — Page
        3 — Document on Disk
        4 — Control Printer
        5 — Type Through
        6 — View Document
        7 — Initialize Printer

Options

        S — Select Printer                        Epson LQ-850
        B — Binding                               0"
        N — Number of Copies                      1
        G — Graphics Quality                      Medium
        T — Text Quality                          High










Selection: 0
```

Fig.2.1 The initial print menu. Some options lead to further menu
        screens.

printer drivers disk is located. If this should happen, select the
appropriate option by pressing key "2", and then type the letter of
the correct drive followed by a colon (e.g. "A:") and then press
"Return".

You must select the printer driver disk which contains the required printer driver. Use printer disk 1 for HP Laserjet or compatible
printers (which means most laser, LED, and LCD printers). Printer
disk 2 is for Postscript compatible printers (the more expensive laser

types) and daisywheel printers. Printer disk 3 contains the dot matrix printer drivers (9 and 24 pin types) while printer disk 4 contains drivers for a range of laser printers. Note that further printer driver disks are available from the Wordperfect Corporation. Details of these can be found on the file called "readme" on printer disk 4 (there is a charge for some of these disks, but several are available free to registered Wordperfect users).

Selecting the right printer driver can be a little confusing. As many printers have their own control code standards, but can also emulate one or more other printers, you could be in the position of having two or more drivers that are compatible with your printer. If there is a driver specifically for your printer, then this is almost certainly the one which will give the best results. However, you can always install all the drivers that are compatible with your printer, and try them in practice to see which, if any, gives the best results.

When the drivers disk has been read you will be presented with a list of the printers it accommodates. The printer at the top of the list will be highlighted, but by using the "up" and "down" cursor keys you can highlight the appropriate printer name and then select it by pressing key "1" (the "Select" option) and then pressing the "Return" key. If the printer you are using is not in the list (or the type it emulates is not listed), you can try another printer disk using option 2 and typing the correct drive identification ("A:" or "B:").

Once you have selected a printer and the driver has been installed, the screen will show some text that will provide helpful information about using your printer with Wordperfect (the correct DIP switch settings to use for example). Just how much information is provided varies a lot from one printer to another. When you have read and digested the information, press "F7" to move on to the printer edit screen (Figure 2.2). This enables you to select such things as the port your printer is connected to, and the size of paper in use.

Option 1 enables you to change the name of the printer as it appears on the printer selection screen. If you are using a printer that is compatible with the named printer, you might prefer to have the name of the printer you are actually using shown on the printer selection screen.

Option 2 is of greater importance, and this tells Wordperfect which port of the computer the printer is connected to. The default

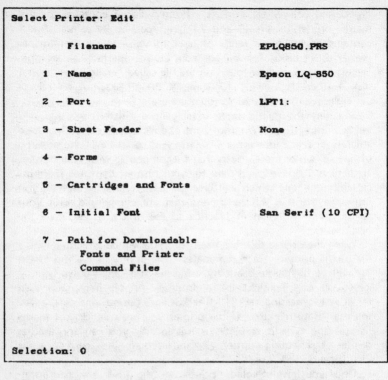

```
Select Printer: Edit

            Filename                    EPLQ850.PRS

     1 - Name                           Epson LQ-850

     2 - Port                           LPT1:

     3 - Sheet Feeder                   None

     4 - Forms

     5 - Cartridges and Fonts

     6 - Initial Font                   San Serif (10 CPI)

     7 - Path for Downloadable
         Fonts and Printer
         Command Files




Selection: 0
```

Fig.2.2   The printer edit screen. With option 2 you can print to any port, or even a named disk file.

is "LPT1:", which might be marked on the computer as printer port 1, parallel port 1, or something along these lines. If your computer only has one parallel printer port, then this will almost certainly be LPT1:. If your printer is connected to printer port 2, then you should change "LPT1:" to "LPT2:". If the printer is connected to serial port 1 (or RS232C port 1), then you should give the port as "COM1:". In the event that your computer only has one serial port, then this should be COM1:. If the printer is connected to serial port 2, then you should specify "COM2:" as the port.

With option 3 you can inform Wordperfect that you are using a sheet feeder (i.e. single sheets of paper automatically fed to the printer from a stack of paper). If you select this option you will be given a list of sheet feeders, and you must then indicate the type you are using. The appropriate printer disk must be accessible to the program, and you may be asked to specify the drive in which the printer disk is located. If you are using continuous stationery, or hand fed single sheets, then this option should be ignored.

Option 4 ("Forms") can not be ignored, as this tells Wordperfect the size and type of paper you are using. When you enter this option you are given three further options, which are to "Add", "Delete", or "Edit" a form description. When initially setting up Wordperfect it is presumably the "Add" option (press the "1" key) that you will require. This leads to a list of form types such as "Standard", and "Envelopes". After choosing the appropriate form type by pressing the corresponding number key, a further list of options is produced.

The first of these is used to select the "Form Size", which is very much like selecting the page size using the "Format" command. Normally the "Form" and "Page" sizes selected using the "Print" and "Format" commands will be the same. Wordperfect will probably refuse to print anything if you should try to use a "form" size that is smaller than the selected "page" size. In option 2 ("Orientation"), "portrait" means that the paper is used upright (i.e. so that it is higher than it is wide). This is the default for most forms, and is obviously the way most documents are produced. "Landscape" orientation is where the paper is turned on its side, so that it is wider than it is high. Obviously you must choose a paper type that is supported by your printer, and Wordperfect will not accept a form that the printer can not handle.

Option 3 ("Initially Present") determines whether Wordperfect starts printing at once when you tell it to print something, or whether you have to go to the printer control screen in order to initiate printing. This option would normally be set to "Yes" for continuous stationery and for a printer fitted with a sheet feeder. In both cases there will normally be paper in the printer all the time, so that it is safe for printing to commence immediately. If sheets are manually fed to the printer one at a time, it is safer to set this option to "No". After issuing a command to print something, you then set up the printer, go to the printer control screen, and then start the printing process.

With option 4 you inform Wordperfect of the type of paper feed in use. This is "Continuous" if you are using a tractor feed unit with continuous stationery, or "Manual" if you are using single sheets and feeding them into the computer by hand. For a sheet feeder the "Bin Number" option is selected, and you type in the appropriate bin number (probably "1") followed by "Return".

The final option ("Page Offsets") enables the printing position to be adjusted so that identical left and right hand margins are obtained, together with the correct spaces at the top and bottom of the page. In many cases this option will not be needed, and can be left at the default settings of 0" and 0". If it is necessary to adjust the printing position on the paper, in most instances this will be accomplished by physically adjusting the position of the paper in the printer. Where this is inappropriate, the "Page Offsets" option might provide an answer. Positive values move the printing position up and to the left — negative values move it in the opposite direction.

More Printers

Once these options have been set, you can save them to disk by repeatedly hitting "F7" until you get back to the initial "Print" menu, or right back to the document screen if preferred. Wordperfect gives great versatility in that it can readily accommodate several printers. These might be connected to different ports of the computer, or could all be connected to the same port via a switch box. Wordperfect can handle it either way, since it lets you specify any valid port for each printer. If you wish to install more than one printer in the program, additional printers are installed by first pressing "Shift" and "F7" to bring up the initial "Print" command menu. Then select option 2 ("Additional Printer;") etc., as for the first printer that was installed.

We have not previously considered the other options available on the "Select Printers" menu, and it is worth doing so now. The first option is "Select;", which is not applicable unless you have more than one printer installed. At the top section of the screen you will notice a list of the installed printers, together with a bullet shown beside one of them. This is the one that is currently selected. One of the printers is highlighted by being shown in reverse video, and by using the up and down cursor keys you can select which of the printers is highlighted in this way. In order to select a new printer, first use the cursor keys to highlight it, and then press key "1" to pick the "Select;" option.

With option 3 ("Edit;") you can edit an existing printer installation. Apart from the fact this operates on an existing setup, it is the same as installing an additional printer. The printer installation that is edited is the one which is highlighted on the screen in reverse video (or some other colour scheme to make it stand out). It is this printer installation definition that is edited, and not the one that is currently selected.

If you wish to have two almost identical printer definitions installed, perhaps because you have two identical printers fitted on different ports, the "Copy;" option is useful. It copies the installation definition for the currently highlighted printer (not the currently selected printer). You can then edit this to change the printer port, or whatever.

Option 5 is used if you wish to delete a printer installation definition, perhaps because you have changed to a new printer. It deletes the currently highlighted printer definition, but only if you press the "Y" key in confirmation. Option 6 is "Help;", which brings up the help screen giving tips for the currently highlighted printer. Option 7 is "Update:", and is selected if you should obtain an improved driver for your printer. Probably you will never need to use this option (refer to page 326 of the Wordperfect manual if you should need to do so).

More Forms

As well as having more than one printer installed, you can also have more than one form definition for each printer. If you go into the main "Print" menu screen, choose the "Select" option, then pick the "Edit;" option for the appropriate printer, and finally select "Forms". This brings up a menu screen that enables you to add, delete, or edit form definitions. Note that you do not use this menu screen to select the required form type for a document. This is handled by the "Format" command. Press "Shift" and "F8" to invoke this command, then select option 2 "Page". Finally, select option 8, "Paper Size/Type", and select the required form type. The "Format" command was described in chapter 1, and will not be considered further at this point. However, some aspects of this command are covered later in this chapter.

Printing Out

Having reached the stage where the printer driver or drivers are fully installed, it is a good idea to type in a short test document and then try to print it out. Starting printing is very easy, and it is just a matter of pressing "Shift" and "F7" to bring up the initial "Print" command menu, and then picking either option 1 ("Full Document") or option 2 ("Page"), depending on whether you wish to print the full document or just one page of it. If you select the "Page" option, the page that is printed is the one in which the cursor currently resides. Of course, if the document is only a single page type, options 1 and 2 have the same effect.

Note that if the driver for your printer is set up so that the printer is not immediately available, this command alone will not initiate printing. All that will happen is a "beep" will be produced from the computer to indicate that it is waiting to be told it is alright to start printing. To give it the go ahead you must first invoke the "Print" command again by pressing "Shift" and "F7". Then choose option 4 ("Control Printer"). This will bring up the printer control screen (Figure 2.3), which should show a message along the lines "Waiting for a Go — press G to continue". If you press the "G" key the printer should commence printing, possibly after a short delay.

If the document is more than one page long the computer will "beep" again when the first page has been printed (or somewhat earlier than this if the printer is fitted with a large memory buffer). Once the first page has been printed and you have inserted a new piece of paper, press the "G" key again to print out the second page. This process is repeated until all the pages have been printed out.

If the printer refuses to do anything, check that it is switched on, and switched on-line. Also check that it is connected to the right port, and the printer driver is set up to use the right port. A common problem when first using a printer is that of it either printing everything on the same line, or double spacing being produced where only single spacing is called for. This is where the program supplies a carriage return and expects the printer to provide the linefeed (but it does not), or the program and the printer both supply a linefeed with each carriage return. With Wordperfect it is the extra spacing that is most likely to occur. This can usually be cured by setting a switch on the printer to the mode where it does not provide a carriage return with each linefeed it receives.

Printer Control
The printer control screen provides access to a number of useful facilities. The first of these is to cancel a print run, or if there are several print jobs queued up, any one or all of them can be cancelled. This would not normally be necessary, but you may wish to

```
Print: Control Printer

Current Job

Job Number: None                              Page Number: None
Job Status: No print jobs                     Current Copy: None
Message:    None
Paper:      None
Location:   None
Action:     None


Job List
Job  Document                  Destination         Print Options


Additional Jobs Not Shown: 0

1 Cancel Job(s); 2 Rush Job; 3 Display Jobs; 4 Go (start printer); 5 Stop:
```

Fig.2.3   The printer control screen. This is especially important if you are using manually fed single sheets in your printer.

53

halt printing if you discover that something has not been set up correctly and the document is not printing out according to plan, or if the paper becomes jammed in the printer perhaps. I have had cause to use this facility on numerous occasions for one reason or another.

You may be puzzled about Wordperfect having a queue of print jobs. With many word processors, and other types of program come to that, if the program is asked to print something out, that is all it can do. Any other tasks have to wait until printing has finished. With Wordperfect printing can be undertaken as a background task. This means that while a document is being printed out, you can still use Wordperfect for word processing. All its facilities are available, but might be noticeably slowed down since the computer's processing power has to be shared between word processing functions and printing. Since all of Wordperfect's facilities remain functioning during printing, it is possible to supply it with further print commands, thus building up a list of print jobs.

The second option is "Rush Job", which enables a print job to be brought to the head of the queue. As only jobs in the print job list can jump the queue, you must put a print job into the queue before it can be brought to the fore. If you select this option, when prompted you must provide the number of the print job to be rushed. You are given the option of having this print job done when the current one has been completed, or the present print job can be interrupted so that printing of the rush job can commence immediately. If this second option is chosen, when the rush job has been completed the previous job will be recommenced from the top of the page that was being printed when the interruption occurred.

"Display Jobs" is the third option. Only three print jobs are shown in the normal job list, but by selecting this option you can display any job in the current list. Pressing any key exits back to the standard printer control display. If there are any jobs not shown on this display, the "Additional Jobs Not Shown:" message below the job list will inform you of how many additional print jobs there are in the queue.

Option 4 is the "Go" command that was described previously. The final option is "Stop:", which has the effect of stopping printing but does not cancel the current print job. This option could be used if (say) printing had to be temporarily stopped while the printer ribbon was changed. Note that many printers have an "off-line" switch, or something similar, and this might be a better way of temporarily halting printing. Many printers have quite large buffers, and this will cause a substantial delay between issuing a "Cancel Job" or "Stop" instruction, and printing actually coming to a halt.

"Print" Menu

There are several commands available on the main "Print" command screen that we have not considered so far. We have considered the subject of printing the current document, or the "screen" in Wordperfect terminology. There is another option available under the "print" command, which is to print a "Document On Disk" (option 3). If you choose this option you will be prompted to supply the filename of the document you wish to print out. This option is more versatile than the screen printing options in that you have the choice of printing the full document, or a selected range of pages (not a limitation of just one page). If the document you wish to print has been formatted for a different printer it can still be printed using the print a "Document On Disk" option, but Wordperfect will warn you that it has been formatted for a different printer.

Remember that a disk file can also be printed out using the "Print;" option of the "List Files" command that was described in chapter 1. This works in much the same way as the "Print" command's "Document On Disk" option, but it provides a more convenient way of finding and selecting the appropriate disk file.

Although there is no print command which enables specified pages of the "screen" to be printed out, it is perhaps worth mentioning that you can print out any part of a document by first selecting it using the "Block" command, then invoking the "Print" command, and then pressing "Y" in response to the on-screen prompt.

Option 5 under the print command is "Type Through". This effectively enables Wordperfect plus a printer to function as a simple electronic typewriter. It may seem strange to want to do this, but the power of Wordperfect is far greater than is needed for some jobs, such as writing a note a few lines long, or addressing the odd envelope here and there. It is also useful for filling out forms, which borders on the impossible with word processing but is reasonably easy with a typewriter or pseudo-typewriter.

When this option is selected there are two sub-options on offer. These are "By Line" and "By Character", and with the latter each character is printed as you type it. With the former, nothing is printed until you reach the end of a line and press "Return". Remember that with a typewriter there is no automatic word-wrapping. With some printers only one of these options may be available (only the "By Line" option is available with my 24 pin dot matrix printer for example), and some printers do not support type-through at all. For form filling the character-by-character method is probably the best, but for other purposes printing line-by-line is better in that it gives you an opportunity to correct typing errors before they are printed out. Press "F7" to exit from the type through facility.

The sixth option is a very useful one which enables you to preview a document on the screen in true WYSIWYG (what you see is what you get) fashion. The normal Wordperfect document screen falls short of being a true WYSIWYG type in several respects. As a few examples, text is not normally shown justified even if it will print out with a justified left hand margin, page numbers are not shown, and graphics are shown as empty boxes. The "Preview" option enables the document to be viewed exactly as it will be printed out, complete with headers, footers, graphics, page numbers, or whatever formatting options you have selected. At least, it will give the most accurate representation that your computer's display card and monitor will permit. High resolution graphics is a definite advantage if you intend to use the "Preview" option a great deal with complex documents. It is important to realise that this facility is only for viewing the document to check that it is formatted correctly — you can not edit it in any way while using the "Preview" option.

Three levels of zoom are provided, and "Full Page" gives the lowest level of zoom, with the whole page being represented on the screen. The "100%" option shows the page at about full size, but will probably display slightly less than the full page. With the "200%" option the page is shown at about twice actual size, and probably only a small part of it will be visible at any one time. You can scroll around the page using the cursor keys, and you can move around the document using the "Pg Up", "Pg Dn", etc. keys. The final option is "Facing Pages", which provides a view of two facing pages on the screen, side-by-side. The "Switch" command ("Shift" plus "F3") toggles a changeover between the display's foreground and background colours. You can therefore have a preview page that matches the real thing (i.e. light background with dark printing) if the screen does not default to this anyway.

The final option under the "Print" heading is "Initialise Printer". This is used if you need to down-load soft fonts to your printer.

Options Options

The "Print" command provides further options under the "Options" heading. The "Select Printers" one has already been considered in some detail. The next option is "Binding", which is used when pages will be bound together. When this is done it is normal to have the printing shifted out from the binding, so that the whole of each page is easily readable. This option enables you to specify the required offset for the printing. The "Number Of Copies" option is self-explanatory — if you wish to print more than one copy of a document you specify the number of copies to be printed using this option.

The "Graphics Quality" setting enables you to select between "Draft;", "Medium;", "High;", and "Do Not Print;". The "High;" option is the one to use when printing out the final versions of documents. The other ones enable the printing process to be speeded up, but the reduced graphics quality (or totally absent graphics) make these options only suitable for checking purposes. Of course, unless a document actually contains some graphics, this option will have no effect on the printing speed.

Under the final option it is possible to select the "Text Quality". This offers the same choices as the "Graphics Quality" option, and is again used to provide increased print speed when printing out draft copies of documents for checking purposes. When using this option you should bear in mind that there can be some inconsistencies between draft and high quality printouts, apart from the differences in quality. The fonts available from some printers are different depending on whether they are used in draft or letter quality mode. Wordperfect will choose the nearest font if the correct one is not available. Also bear in mind that print quality settings are not applicable to all printers. With a daisywheel printer for instance, the print quality is determined by the type of ribbon and paper used, not by the printer itself. Not all dot matrix printers support three print qualities, although most do these days.

Formatting

So far we have covered the process of getting your text into Wordperfect, and printing it out. However, simply typing in a document and printing it out might not give exactly the desired result. You may need to use some further facilities of Wordperfect in order to get things such as the line spacing and page numbering correct. These facilities are under the control of the "Format" command. Some of the facilities this command provides have already been covered, but there are a number which have not, but which will be covered here. Figure 2.4 helps to illustrate some of these points.

```
Format: Line


    1 — Hyphenation                          Off

    2 — Hyphenation Zone — Left              10%
                          Right              4%

    3 — Justification                        Yes

    4 — Line Height                          Auto

    5 — Line Numbering                       No

    6 — Line Spacing                         1

    7 — Margins — Left                       1"
                  Right                      1"

    8 — Tab Set                              0", every 0.5"

    9 — Widow/Orphan Protection              No


Selection: 0
```

Fig.2.4   The line format screen. Line spacing and justification are
just two of the features controlled via this menu.

With some of these formatting commands you might find it easier to place them into the document as you type it. With others you

58

might find it easier to add them once the document is in other respects finished, and ready to be printed out. Line spacing is certainly one that I would suggest should be left until it is time to print out the document. If you set double or triple line spacing, this will affect the spacing of both the display and the printed out document. As a result of this you will find that there are relatively few lines of text shown on the screen, which could make editing the document more difficult. In order to set the line spacing, first invoke the "Format" command by pressing "Shift" and "F8". Select option 1 ("Line") which will then bring up a further full page menu display. Then select option 6 ("Line Spacing;") and enter the number of linefeeds that should be added at the end of each line. Then press "Return" followed by "F7" (twice) in order to return to the document screen (which should reflect the line spacing you have set).

Note that the line spacing can be altered at any point in the document. To set the line spacing for the entire document, make sure that the cursor is placed at the very beginning of the document before using the line spacing command. You can make sure the cursor is at the beginning of the document by pressing "Home" twice followed by the "up" cursor key. Incidentally, if you press "Home" three times and then press the left cursor key, this takes the cursor right to the beginning of the line, even placing it prior to any control codes. However, it is not normally necessary to do this.

Hyphenation
There are some other useful formatting commands available under the "Line" menu. Hyphenation (option 1) can be switched on so that long words at the end of a line are automatically split over two lines, rather than being placed entirely on the second line. The difference between the "Manual;" and "Auto;" options is that in the manual mode you are asked to confirm each hyphenation. Press "Esc" to confirm hyphenation, or "F1" to cancel it. In the automatic hyphenation mode Wordperfect uses a set of rules to control the way in which it hyphenates words. If its rules can not cope with a situation, it temporarily switches to manual mode.

If you do any manual hyphenation there are four types of hyphen available to you, only two of which will normally be needed. One of these is the hard hyphen, which is simply the hyphen ("-") character, which is treated and printed out like any other character. Remember when using this character it will always be displayed on the screen and printed even if some text is deleted or added, thus moving it from the end of a line. A soft hyphen is the type that Wordperfect puts into a word, and it is displayed on the screen if it is in the hyphenation zone. Pressing "Ctrl" and "-" will place a soft hyphen in a document. The hyphenation zone is controlled by option 2, and a word is hyphenated if it begins within the left hyphenation zone and goes beyond the right zone. It is probably best to leave the default settings unless you have problems with automatic hyphenation.

Justification

The default is for justification of the right hand margin to be switched on. Wordperfect then adds spaces into each line to ensure that its length exactly equals the maximum number of characters per line, giving a neat right hand margin. Option 3 enables justification to be toggled. Note that in order to speed up reformatting of text the document screen is not justified (but the preview screen is justified).

The "Line Height" option, as its name suggests, enables you to set the height of each line. There would normally be no need to do this, as Wordperfect will always choose something sensible for the font in use. The next option permits lines to be numbered in a number of user selectable styles, but this is probably something that few users will have much need for. All the other "Line" options have been covered previously, and will not be dealt with again here.

Page Format

There are several important features of Wordperfect that are accessed via the "Page" option of the "Format" command. Figure 2.5 shows the menu that appears when the "Page" option is selected. The more minor options include "Centre Page (top to bottom)", which does exactly that when the document is printed out, and "Force Odd/Even Page". The latter simply ensures that the page on which the cursor resides is odd or even (whichever you select), with a blank page being inserted if necessary.

"Headers" and "Footers" rank among the more important of the "Page" options. This facility enables a piece of text to be printed at the top or bottom of every page. There is a separate page numbering facility, but the page numbers can be included in headers and footers by typing "^B". The "Headers" and "Footers" options permit the text to be included on every page, only on odd pages, or

```
Format: Page

    1  -  Centre Page (top to bottom)      No

    2  -  Force Odd/Even Page

    3  -  Headers

    4  -  Footers

    5  -  Margins - Top                     1"
                    Bottom                  1"

    6  -  New Page Number                   1
          (example: 3 or iii)

    7  -  Page Numbering                    No page numbering

    8  -  Paper Size                        8.5" x 11"
          Type                              Standard

    9  -  Suppress (this page only)

Selection: 0
```

Fig.2.5   The page format menu screen.

only on even pages. You can, of course, produce separate headers and footers for odd pages and even pages. There is a "Discontinue" option that permits headers and footers to be switched off. Before selecting this option place the cursor in the first page where you wish the headers and footers to cease. Most of Wordperfect's facilities are available when producing headers and footers (there are a few restrictions which are mainly inconsequential), and the spelling checker will check both headers and footers. They are not normally displayed on the screen, but the "Reveal Codes" command will show up the first fifty characters. Headers and footers are, of course, shown on pages displayed using the "Preview" command.

Option 6 enables a new page number to be selected. This is mainly used when a document is being produced as separate files (this book was produced with each chapter as a separate file for example). The default page numbering is fine for the first section of the document, but subsequent sections will start from page 1, rather than starting out where the previous section left off. This option enables you to start the page number at the appropriate figure. You select Arabic or Roman numerals by typing in the new page number in the appropriate form. This facility can be used to switch from the default (Arabic) numbering to Roman numerals if required.

Page numbering is enabled and disabled using option 7. If page numbering is switched on, there are various positioning options available. A "map" appears on screen which helpfully shows which page position each option number corresponds to. As mentioned previously, you can insert the page number into headers and footers by typing "^B". This will also work in the main body of the text, but is perhaps less useful in this context.

Fonts
For most purposes the standard font (size and style of lettering), plus bold and underlined versions of it, will suffice. However, many printers these days support a variety of fonts and printing effects, and Wordperfect provides a facility that enables you to switch fonts etc. as and when necessary. Just how useful (or otherwise) this feature will be depends on what printer you are using, and the range of fonts and printing effects it supports. It might be of limited use with a daisywheel printer, where changes in font are normally accomplished by changing the print wheel. Most modern dot matrix printers are well endowed with a range of fonts and

printing effects, but an inexpensive dot matrix printer that is several years old might have very limited capabilities.

If you are using a Wordperfect printer driver that is for a compatible printer, rather than one which is specifically designed for your type of printer, bear in mind that the compatibility might only be partial. Some of the fonts and effects might not be available on your printer, or might not give quite the desired effect. The same is also true if you are using a Wordperfect printer driver for a printer that is an up-dated version of the one you are using. A further point to bear in mind is that some of the fonts and effects might only be available if the printer is fitted with the appropriate add-on font cartridge, or some other add-on device or software.

Font changing is a two-tier process, where you can select a "base" font, and then have several variations on that font (such as letter size, shadow effect printing, etc.). In order to select the required base font you first invoke the "Font" command by pressing "Ctrl" and "F8". Then select option 4 ("Base Font;"), which will produce a list of available fonts on the screen. You can scroll through these using the "up" and "down" cursor keys to highlight the one you require. This is then selected by pressing the "1" key. The currently selected font is marked with a "*" character incidentally.

Variations on the base font are selected by invoking the "Font" command by pressing the "Ctrl" and "F8" keys, and then selecting option 1 ("Size;") or option 2 ("Appearance;"). The "Size;" option gives access to such things as superscript, subscript, and large letters. The "Appearance;" option enables bold and underlining to be selected, but note that these are available using the corresponding Wordperfect commands. Other effects are also available via this option, including some that can not be obtained via other commands (italic lettering and shadow effect printing). In order to switch back to the standard base font you must first invoke the "Font" command by pressing "Ctrl" and "F8", and then select option 3 ("Normal;").

Font changes can be placed into the text as you type a document, or they can be added in afterwards. The "Font" command can also be used in conjunction with the "Block" command, and this represents an easy way of setting the required font for small or large pieces of text. Remember to define the block of text before you invoke the "Font" command. Only the "Size;" and "Appearance;" options are available when the "Font" command is used in this way.

If you intend to make use of the "Font" command it is a good idea to produce a trial document having various fonts, sizes of lettering, and printing effects. You can then judge which fonts, effects, etc., are best suited to particular applications.

Finally

This does not cover all the available options when formatting a document ready for printing, but it does cover most of them. It also covers the ones that you are most likely to need. It is worthwhile looking through the other "Format" command menus to see if there is anything there that will enable you to print the document in a form that is more to your liking.

Chapter 3

ADVANCED FEATURES

Wordperfect is not exactly short of advanced features, and it contains what are in some cases virtually separate programs run from within the main program. The advanced features of Wordperfect include the spelling checker, thesaurus, mail-merge and sort commands, and the ability to include graphics within documents. There is insufficient space available to consider all the advanced features Wordperfect has to offer, but we look in some detail at the ones mentioned above, which are probably the ones that are most frequently used by the bulk of Wordperfect users.

Spell Checking
The spelling checker function of Wordperfect is one of the best available. It has a massive dictionary of around 120,000 words, which is an important factor. Spelling checkers with dictionaries that are substantially smaller than this tend to be difficult to use as they turn up large numbers of (supposedly) incorrectly spelled words. What a spelling checker program actually does is to compare each word in your document with the words in its dictionary in an attempt to find a match for each one. If it can not find a match, then the word is assumed to be incorrectly spelled, and the program points the word out to you.

In reality it could be that the word is perfectly correct, but that it is not in the spelling checker's dictionary for some reason. Most dictionaries (electronic or otherwise) miss out at least a few common words, or variations on some common words (plurals for instance). You can not reasonably expect a spelling checker to have a lot of unusual technical terms or abbreviations in its dictionary. Putting too many words in the dictionary could be counterproductive with virtually everything, right or wrong, being matched with a word in the dictionary. What you can reasonably expect, and what Wordperfect permits, is for you to customise the dictionary by adding to it any common words you discover are missing from the main dictionary, or any technical terms or abbreviations you will be using.

To be strictly accurate about it, these words are not added to the main dictionary, but are put into a supplementary dictionary. Wordperfect actually uses a three-tier system of checking in order to make the process as fast as possible. Each word is first checked against a dictionary of common words. If that fails it is then checked against the main dictionary, and if no match is found there it is checked against your supplementary dictionary. If that fails, the word is pointed out to you.

What you do about the (possibly) incorrectly spelled word is then up to you. You can simply leave it as it is if it is correct, but is something too obscure to be in Wordperfect's dictionary. You can add the word to the supplementary dictionary, or not bother if you feel it is not worthwhile doing so. One of the more advanced aspects of Wordperfect's spelling checker is that it offers some words which it feels could be the one you require. This is done on the basis of choosing words in its dictionary that have spellings which almost match the word in question. It is up to you whether or not you accept one of these alternatives. The number offered varies enormously depending on how many words in the dictionary happen to be similar to the misspelled word. There may be no similar words, or there could be dozens of them. Another option offered by the spelling checker is to manually edit the word. In fact this is the only satisfactory option available to you if the word is incorrect but no alternatives are offered by the program.

Do not fall into the trap of getting the spelling checker to do all the checking for you. It is far from 100% reliable in that it will accept any word that it finds in its dictionary. There is a real risk of words being overlooked by the spelling checker if you have accidentally hit the wrong key when typing in a word, but have produced a word that does exist. There are numerous common examples of wrong words that are produced in this way, and my one finger typing is very good at producing "of" when I meant to type "or". The "F" key is immediately below the "R" key and it is easy to miss one and hit the other. If accuracy in a document is important, read it through thoroughly and correct it yourself first. Then use the spelling checker to search for any mistakes you have missed.

As well as being much quicker and easier than using an ordinary dictionary to check the spelling of any words you are uncertain about, a spelling checker should also significantly improve the accuracy of your work. The words you know you can not spell you look up in the dictionary and get right. The ones that cause the problem are the words that you think you can spell but are getting wrong. With a spelling checker program you are effectively looking up in the dictionary all the words you type, and any you think you can spell but can not will be pointed out to you. When checking a document it is very difficult to spot every little mistake. Most computer displays are somewhat less legible than the printed out documents, which increases the chances of minor mistakes getting through to the printed out documents. Again, as the spelling checker meticulously checks every word, and has no problem in accurately reading them all, it should pick up any minor slips. Note that the Wordperfect spelling checker is a so-called "on-line" type. This simply means that you do not have to use it to check the document, but can use it to look up the spelling of a word while you are typing in a document.

In Use

If you wish to use the spelling checker to look up a word you have just typed in, position the cursor anywhere on that word and then press "Ctrl" and "F2" to start the spelling checker. This assumes that Wordperfect is being run from a hard disk. If you are using a floppy disk system you must remove the program disk from drive A and replace it with the spelling checker disk in order to use the spelling checker facility. Once into the spelling checker command, select option 1 ("Word") by pressing the "1" key. If nothing much happens, then the spelling checker has found a match for the word and it is correctly spelled. If the word does not match one in the dictionary, the message "Not Found;" is shown on the status line together with a range of six options.

In the current context not all of these options do anything worthwhile. If you decide to leave the word as it is, even though no match is found, press key "1" to accept the "Skip Once;" option. If you should decide that the word is legitimate and that you wish to add it to the supplementary dictionary, then select option 3 ("Add;").

In order to try another spelling choose option 5 ("Look Up;") and type in the new attempt at the word. When using the spelling checker Wordperfect goes into a split screen mode, with your document in the top section of the screen and the lower section used to display suggested words. If when first checking the word Wordperfect had not found a match, but had found one or more similar words, these would have been listed in the lower section of the screen. In order to select one of the suggested words and have it replace the misspelled word, it is merely necessary to press the key corresponding to the letter shown alongside the word. The spelling checker operates a bit differently in the "Look Up" mode. If nothing is displayed in the lower section of the screen this does not mean that a match was found. It means that not only was a match not achieved, no very similar words were found either. If your word was located it will be displayed in the lower section of the screen. Whether or not it was located, any very similar words in the dictionary will be shown on the screen. You can either select one of these to replace the misspelled word, or go back to the main spelling checker options by pressing "F7".

If you wish to use the spelling checker to check a page of your document, or the entire document, you again invoke the spelling checker command by pressing "Ctrl" and "F2". This time you select option 2 ("Page;") or option 3 ("Document;"), as required. The page or entire document is then checked word by word until it has been completely checked, or (more probably) a suspected error is located. If a suspected error is detected, you get a list of suggested words in the lower window of the display, and the six options mentioned previously are offered on the status display together with the "Not Found;" message. As before, you can use option 1 to continue without changing the word. Alternatively, option 2 will have the same result, except that it will skip over any further occurrences of the same word. In effect, the word is added to the supplementary dictionary, but only until the current spelling checking session has been completed.

Option 3 is again available if you wish to permanently add a word to the supplementary dictionary. Also as before, the "Edit;" facility is available if you wish to manually correct the word, and the "Look Up;" facility is available as option 5. The Wordperfect default is to include words that contain numbers in the checking process. This is undesirable in that a date like the "12th December 1989" will result in "12th" being picked up as an error when it is obviously quite correct. On the other hand, if Wordperfect is set to the "Ignore Numbers;" mode (option 6) it will accept something like "12th", but it will also overlook an error of the type where you have accidentally pressed a number key instead of a letter key (e.g. "th5ee" instead of "three"). It is up to you to select the "Ignore Numbers;" mode if your work will contain a lot of words which contain a mixture of numbers and letters. If not, then it is probably best to ignore this option, and correct any errors that this throws up, or skip over any correct words that are queried. Not using the "Ignore Numbers;" option is always the safest course of action, but with some types of document is could produce so many queried but correct words that it would be impractical. Note that Wordperfect always ignores words that only contain numbers, such as "1989" in our previous example. Do not forget that you can add words (or any sequence of printable characters) to the supplementary dictionary, and although adding a large number of words containing letters and numbers could take a fair amount of time initially, once the task was completed it would permit rapid and accurate checking of documents that would otherwise be difficult to check comprehensively.

From time to time you might find that you have accidentally added a word into the supplementary dictionary that is spelled incorrectly. Although Wordperfect's spelling checker does not provide a facility for removing words from the supplementary dictionary, it is quite easy to do so. If you are using a hard disk system you will find a file called "WP{WP}UK.SUP" in the Wordperfect directory. For a floppy disk system it will be found on the "Speller" disk. Note though, that this file is not initially present, and is generated when you first start adding words to the supplementary dictionary. This file can be loaded into Wordperfect and edited, including deleting any words that have been added in error. The words are sorted into alphabetical order, which should make it easy to rapidly locate a word you wish to remove. The modified file is saved to disk in the usual manner.

Although Wordperfect has no built-in commands for maintaining the dictionary, there is a file called "SPELL.EXE" on the "Speller" disk, which is a utility program for this purpose. The main dictionary can not be properly loaded into Wordperfect itself incidentally, because the data is stored on disk in a compressed format, not in ASCII or standard Wordperfect 5.0 format. Probably most users, even those who use the spelling checker a great deal, will not need to make use of the "Spell" utility program.

Further Features
There are a couple of spelling checker options which we have not considered so far, and these are both on the initial list of options when "Ctrl" and "F2" are pressed. Option 4 ("New Sup. Dictionary.") enables a different supplementary dictionary file to be used. You might like to have several supplementary dictionaries, with a different one being used for each type of document. This is

probably only worthwhile if these dictionaries are of a substantial size, as the increase in checking speed will otherwise not be worthwhile. You might just as well have one supplementary dictionary containing all your additional words. If you use this option, you are prompted for the "Supplementary dictionary name:". The full filename including extension must be provided, as must the drive and path specification if the file is not in the default drive/path.

Option 6 is the "Word Count;" feature. If selected, this results in a "Please Wait" message followed shortly afterwards by the number of words in the document. Wordperfect does not provide a running count of the number of words in a document, and a word count can only be obtained via the spelling checker. Incidentally, if you spell check a page or document, at the end of the checking process Wordperfect will report the number of words in the page or document.

If you only require a rough estimate of the number of words in a document there are several ways of doing this. One is to do an accurate word count on some fairly long documents. You can then work out from this the average number of words you get on a page. Multiplying this figure by the number of pages you have done will then give a rough estimate of the number of words in the document. Another method is to use the "List Files" command to show the length of a document file. Dividing this by six will give a rough indication of the number of words present in the document. The Wordperfect word count operates quite quickly, and except when you are dealing with very long documents it will not take up much time to do regular word counts as you work on a document. It typically takes a little over one second to count 1000 words on a 12MHz "turbo" IBM AT compatible computer.

In common with a number of modern spelling checkers, Wordperfect's spelling checker will detect double occurrences of words. When typing fast it is easy to accidentally type a word twice from time to time. The mistake is sometimes quite obvious when you are checking through a document, but some double words can be surprisingly difficult to spot (particularly when one occurrence is at the end of a line, and the second occurrence is at the beginning of the next line).

If Wordperfect detects the occurrence of a double word it highlights the words in the upper part of the screen and offers a list of four options (numbered "2" to "5"). Option 2 ("Skip;") is used if the double occurrence is correct, and the program then simply carries on with the spelling checking. Option 3 is "Delete 2nd;", and it results in the second occurrence of the word being deleted. Option 4 enables you to "Edit;" the document, and this is the option to use if one of the words is wrong. For example, if you typed "then then" instead of "then they", the "Edit;" option enables you to change the second "then" to "they". The final option is "Disable Double Word Checking;", which does exactly what it says. This option would not normally be used, but could be useful if the document is a table, list, or something of this nature, which correctly has a large number of double word occurrences.

Users of Wordperfect 4.2 and earlier issues of the program should note that the command structure for the spelling checker is a little different with these versions of the program. The differences are actually quite minor, apart from one facility which would seem to be totally absent from Wordperfect 5.0. The phonetic look up option (which enables you to search for a word that sounds like your word, but does not necessarily have a similar spelling) seems to be absent from Wordperfect 5.0. However, it is still available as option 8 in the "SPELL" utility program. Possibly this option is missing due to Wordperfect including a phonetic element in its main spelling checker routine. For example, if you get the spelling checker to check the word "phish", it will offer three words beginning with "f", including "fish".

Some word processors are equipped with spelling checkers that are very slow in operation, inconvenient to operate, and which in practice probably receive very little use. The Wordperfect spelling checker is definitely one of the best spelling checkers in terms of both speed and ease of use. It is well worthwhile using it on all your documents, which will probably be genuinely word perfect as a result.

I should perhaps point out that Wordperfect is produced in the U.S.A., and that its dictionary therefore includes a lot of American spellings for English words. The dictionary has been anglicised though (provided you have the proper U.K. version of the program), and in general the English spellings are present as well. From time to time you might find that the American spelling of a word is the only one present though. This is easily rectified by adding the English spelling to the supplementary dictionary using the "Add;" option.

Thesaurus

The thesaurus can be used to find words that have a similar meaning to a specified word. In other words, it provides a list of synonyms. In the case of the Wordperfect thesaurus, and where appropriate, it also provides an antonym for the specified word. It is possible to look up synonyms of most synonyms, synonyms of most of those synonyms, and so on. You can even look up synonyms of the antonyms in most cases.

The main use of a thesaurus is to find alternative words when you find that you are using the same word over and over again, and if you need a few alternatives in order to reduce the amount of repetition. It has other uses though. If you can not think of a suitable word, you may be able to obtain one from the thesaurus by looking up a word that has a vaguely similar meaning, and then going on to synonyms of synonyms until you gradually home in on a suitable word. Another method is to look up a word that has the opposite meaning to the one you require. You can then find some suitable words by looking up synonyms of the antonym supplied by the program. The Wordperfect thesaurus is based on quite a large dictionary of words, but do not be surprised if you supply it with an obscure or unusual word, and it fails to supply any synonyms. Also, while some words have many synonyms (little and large for instance), there are many words for which there is no reasonably similar alternative.

To use the thesaurus facility you press "Alt" and "F1". If you are running Wordperfect from floppy disks rather than a hard disk, the thesaurus disk must be placed in drive A in order to use this facility. This does not bring up the usual options, but instead results in the screen being divided into two windows. The smaller one at the top is used for the document, while the one at the bottom is divided into three columns, and is used to display synonyms and antonyms. The status line has the prompt — "Word:". You simply type in the word you want to look up, and then press the "Return" key. If the word is within Wordperfect's repertoire it will respond with a list of synonyms plus one or more antonyms where appropriate. The status line will offer a range of options. If the cursor is on a word when you invoke the thesaurus, Wordperfect will assume that this is the word you wish to look up, and it will go straight into this second stage of the operation.

As you will soon discover when you try the "Thesaurus" command, the words provided are sorted into subgroups. Many words have more than one meaning, and so the synonyms are grouped accordingly, where necessary. An "a", "n", or "v" in brackets beside each headword shows whether it is an adjective, noun, or verb (respectively). If a word can operate in more than one category, separate lists of words will be provided for each one, possibly with each one having its own subgroups.

The first of the options you are provided with is "Replace Word;". If you select this option by pressing key "1", Wordperfect will respond with the message "Press letter for word;". You will notice that alongside each word in the first column there is a letter ("A", "B", "C", etc.). Simply press the letter key for the word you want to insert into your text in place of the original word. If the cursor was not on a word when the "Thesaurus" command was invoked, the word you select will be placed at the current cursor position. If there are a lot of synonyms, the word you require might be in column two or column three. To select a word from one of these columns press the right cursor key once or twice, to move the identification letters across to the column in which the desired word appears.

Option 2 ("View Doc;") places the cursor in the upper window and enables you to scroll through the document. The top window in which the document appears remains quite small though (typically just five lines, one of which is used for the status line). This option does not permit any editing of the document — you can only view it. To return to the "Thesaurus" command you simply press "F7".

With option 3 ("Look up word;") you can look up a word that you type in, or one of the synonyms displayed on the screen. To look up a synonym on the screen you first press key "3" to select the "Look up word" option. Then you press the letter key which corresponds to the letter displayed on the left hand side of the word, and press the "Return" key. Alternatively, just press the appropriate letter key without first pressing key "3".

Note that you can only look up synonyms of words that are marked with a bullet (a small dot beside the word). In Wordperfect terminology these are the "headwords". Note also that it is possible to look up synonyms of an antonym provided it is marked with a bullet. Obviously antonyms are inappropriate for some words, and none will be shown. In other cases several antonyms may be shown. If the word you wish to look up is not in the column which has the identifying letters, use the cursor keys to move the letters to the appropriate column. If you wish to look up a synonym for a word that is not displayed in one of the columns, start by pressing the "3" key, as before. However, you should then type in the word you wish to look up, and then press the "Return" key. Either a list of synonyms will be displayed, or the status line will show the message "Word not found;".

If you look up synonyms for two or three words you will probably find that existing information prevents some of the new words from being displayed. To make room for all the new information you can use the "Clear Column;" option. Move the identification letters to the column you wish to clear by using the left and right cursor keys. Then press the "Delete", "Backspace", or "4" key. If you obtain synonyms for three words, it is likely that a lot of the available information will not be shown on the screen. However, you can scroll the information in each column by first using the left and right cursor keys to move the identification letters to the column you wish to examine. Then use the up and down cursor keys to scroll the column until it shows the information you require. The "Page Up" and "Page Down" keys provide a quick means of moving to the top and bottom (respectively) of a column that contains a long list of words.

To exit from the thesaurus you simply press "F7". If you are only going to use Wordperfect for very short documents, the thesaurus will probably be of little or no value to you. On the other hand, if you are involved in the production of documents of a thousand or more words in length, the thesaurus can be of great help. I can not claim to use this facility very often, but it is usually of great help when I do use it.

Sorting

With a lot of word processors there is no built-in sort command at all, or one is included, but is rather limited in its scope. The sort routine available in Wordperfect is a very powerful one, and seems to compare very favourably with many dedicated sort programs. For those who are unfamiliar with the computer term "sort", it should perhaps be explained that this is a facility which sorts words, lines, paragraphs, or whatever, into alphabetical order. Typical applications of a sort routine would be to put the index of a book or a glossary into alphabetical order. Obviously you can manually sort entries into alphabetical order as they are entered, but it is much easier to type them as they come, and then have the computer sort them into the correct order for you. This can save a tremendous amount of time as well as ensuring that there are no errors in the order of the entries.

Before describing a couple of ways in which the sort routine can be used, I must point out that an error when using the sort command could result in your document being scrambled to the point where there would be very little chance of ever getting it un-sorted back to its former state so that you could try again. Before using this command, or any other command that could drastically change the document being edited, always save the document to disk. If the document should become seriously scrambled you can then exit the document without saving it to disk, and then load the non-scrambled version from disk so that you can try again.

The sort command is invoked by pressing "Ctrl" and "F9" (this command is called "Merge/Sort" on the Wordperfect template). Press the "2" key to select the "sort;" option, and then press the "Return" key if you wish to sort the current document. If you wish to sort a file that is on disk, enter its full name etc. and press "Return". If the output of the sort command must go to the screen, press "Return" in response to the next prompt. If the output must go to a file, type in the file name and then press the "Return" key. Note that you can use the "Block" command in conjunction with the "Sort" routine. If a block is marked and the "Sort" command is invoked, the input and output of the sort routine will respectively be the block, and the section of the document occupied by that block.

Having specified the source and output for the sort routine you should be provided with a list of seven options along the status line. The sort routine is a complex one which we will not consider in full detail here. Consequently, some of the options available will not be described here. In addition to the status line, the main screen should go into split operation with the document in the upper window, and information about the options selected being shown in the lower window.

Option 1 ("Perform Action;") actually starts the sorting routine, and it does so without asking for confirmation from the user. You must therefore make quite sure that any necessary setting up of the "Sort" command is done before you select this option. In the mean time, be careful not to accidentally press the "1" key, and remember the warning given above about always saving the document prior to using the "Sort" command.

With option 2 ("View;") you can view the document in the upper window. This operates in much the same way as the "View;" option of the thesaurus. Option 6 ("Order;") enables you to have the entries sorted into either ascending or descending order. The default is descending, which is the usual A, B, C, and 0 to 9 sorting. Choosing an ascending sort results in the entries being placed in reverse alphabetical and numeric order (Z, Y, X, etc.).

With option 7 you can choose between two types of sorting: line and paragraph. Line sorting is the default, and is the one that would be used for something like an index where each entry consists of just one line, each one on a separate line. As far as the sort routine is concerned, it makes no difference whether a line is terminated by a hard return or a soft return — either way each line counts as a separate record. In other words, whether you terminate a line by pressing the "Return" key (hard return), or Wordperfect ends the line by word-wrapping it (soft return), each line on the screen counts as a separate line for sorting purposes. If you wish to sort long lines, this would presumably be possible provided you first set a wide page size, and then reverted to the normal page size.

If you wish to use paragraph sorting, then each paragraph must end with at least two hard returns. In practice this means that you must leave at least one blank line between each paragraph. Leaving no blank lines between paragraphs and indenting the first line of each one will not enable the sort routine to distinguish one paragraph from another. As far as the sort program is concerned, a piece of text of this type is just one long paragraph, and as such will not be affected by a paragraph sort command.

There is actually a third option under "Type;", which is the "Merge;" one. Some information on Wordperfect's "Merge" command (a facility better known as "Mail Merge") is given in the next section of this chapter. Merge sorting will not be discussed further here.

Mail-Merge

Mail-merge is one of the most important functions provided by a word processor, and one that is much exploited by many businesses. Its main use is to enable a standard letter to be produced, and then automatically customised so that each person receiving a letter has one with their name etc., rather than just an impersonal "Dear Customer", "Dear Sir Or Madam", etc. In other words, everyone receiving the letter seems to be receiving an individually typed letter rather than a mass produced one, whereas the reality of the situation is somewhere between these two situations.

In order to use the mail-merge facility you must first have two files available. The first of these is called the "primary" file, and this is your standard letter or other standard document into which names, addresses, etc. must be merged. The second file, called the "secondary" file, is the list of names, addresses, or whatever, that must be merged into the standard document.

It is probably best to start by considering the secondary file, since the logical method of working is to first produce your list of names and addresses and to then produce the primary files into which these must be merged, as and when necessary. Obviously you can not simply produce a long list of names, addresses, telephone numbers, and other information, and expect Wordperfect to sort out for itself just what should go where in the primary file. At the very least you must divide the list into separate "records" by inserting the appropriate merge codes into the document.

In most cases things will not be as simple as this, because you will wish to merge two or more pieces of information into each standard document. For example, you might want to have a name inserted near the beginning of the document, a telephone number somewhere in the middle, and an address at the end. In order to achieve this each record must be divided into separate fields, and in our example above each record would need to be divided into three fields (name, address, and telephone number). This dividing of a record into fields is achieved by placing the appropriate merge code at the appropriate points in each record.

The merge code used to separate records is ^E followed by a hard page. This code is added into the document by pressing "Shift" and "F9" to bring up a list of merge codes along the status line. Pressing the "E" key inserts both the ^E code and the hard page code into the document. To separate fields within a record you use the ^R merge code. This can be obtained simply by pressing the "F9" key.

In order to try out the mail-merge facility, produce a file called "secfile" which contains three or four names, addresses, and telephone numbers. Type in the first name followed by a ^R, then the first address followed by another ^R, and then the telephone number followed by both a ^R and a ^E. Repeat this process for the other two or three records.

You then need a primary file into which you can merge some or all the fields of the secondary file. For the purposes of trial run type in the dummy letter shown below:—

123 Dummy Street,
Anytown,
Somethingshire,
WP5 5WP.
2nd May 1989.

Dear ^F1^

You are cordially invited to my 150th birthday party on the 20th June next at this address. Proceedings start at 8-00pm, and fancy dress is compulsory (so your normal attire should be suitable).

Sincere regards.

Yours,

J. Smith.

^F2^

The fields in a secondary file are numbered, starting at the top and working downwards. Therefore, in our "secfile" example the name is field one, the address is field 2, and the telephone number is field 3. It is possible to name fields using the ^N merge code, but unless you are using a large number of fields it is probably not worthwhile bothering with this feature. In this example letter we are just using field numbers where data from the secondary file must be merged with the primary file. To indicate that a field must be merged into the primary file you use the ^F option of the "Merge Codes" command. Press "Shift" and "F9" to invoke this command, and then press the "F" key to select the ^F merge code. You will then be prompted at the status line to enter the field number. This is field 1 at the point in the letter where the name must merge, and field 2 where the address must be included in the primary file. There is no need to make use of all the fields in a secondary file, and in this case we are not bothering to include field 3 (the telephone number). When you have completed the dummy letter, save it as a file called "primfile". Then exit this document, but do not exit Wordperfect.

You have now reached the stage where the mail-merge feature can be tried out. To invoke the "Merge" command press "Ctrl" and "F9". In response to the prompt on the status line, give "primfile" as the primary file name and press "Return". In response to the next prompt give "secfile" as the secondary file name. In both cases, where appropriate any drive name and path specification should be included. Wordperfect should then return to the document screen with the cursor at the bottom of a document that consists of the three or four correctly mail-merged letters. These can be edited in the normal way if necessary.

There can be a few minor problems when you start using a mail-merge facility, such as duplications of spaces, punctuation marks, and carriage returns, or some of these being missing. This is just a matter of standardising things so that you always include these in the primary file or the secondary file, not neither or both. There can be a problem with unwanted blank lines appearing in a document where you have asked for a field to be merged, but that field is empty. In our names, addresses, and telephone numbers example, you might not have a telephone number for everyone included in the file. If a field is empty, you must still include it as a blank line in the secondary file. If you do not, this will upset the field numbering for the file and things could go drastically wrong. In order to avoid unwanted blank lines caused by empty fields being merged, add a question mark at the end of the field merge code (e.g "^F2?").

The mail-merged letters are in the form of one long document, whereas, on the face of it, you need several separate documents. The fact that the letters are in one document should not give any problems in practice since a hard page control character is placed between each letter. Therefore, if you print out the document, the letters will be printed on separate pages.

Before putting together large secondary files with numerous names, addresses, etc. you need to give careful thought to how the fields are organised. To give maximum versatility you should use several fields rather than lumping everything together as a single entity. In our example we used separate fields for the name, address, and telephone number, which is far more useful than having all three together as a single field. It might be better to use even

79

more fields, with (say) the post code having its own field. In use it might be more convenient to have records split over several files rather than put together in one large file. Categorising the records will make it easier to do selective mail-merging. Also, if you have a large number of records and a large document to merge them into, there is a risk of the computer running out of memory. Doing several smaller mail-merge and printing runs reduces the risk of any problems due to inadequate memory. As you may have already gathered, records can be sorted using the "Merge;" option available under the "Type;" option of the "Sort" command.

There are a number of facilities available under the mail-merge feature which have not been considered here, and which can not be dealt with due to lack of available space. For many purposes the basic facilities described here are all that are needed. However, if you are going to make extensive use of the mail-merge facility it is well worth studying the relevant section of the Wordperfect manual to see if any of the other features available are likely to be of value to you. Once you understand the basic way in which mail-merging is handled it is not difficult to get to grips with the finer points of this command.

Graphics

The main difference between Wordperfect version·4.2 and version 5.0 is that the latter can import graphics into documents. Provided you have a suitable printer, the graphics will be included on print-outs and will be of good quality. It is important to realise that Wordperfect does not itself have any proper drawing commands. There are some basic line drawing facilities, but nothing that would really justify a claim to graphics capabilities. If you wish to use graphics in documents there are two basic choices. One of these is to use pre-drawn artwork, or "clip art" as it is generally known. Commercial, shareware, and public domain clip art can be obtained, and Wordperfect can handle drawing files in a number of popular formats. Some sample clip art is provided as part of the Wordperfect 5.0 package.

The second method is to produce your own drawings using a computer aided drawing (CAD) or paint program, depending on the type of illustration you require. The drawing files, provided they are in a suitable format, can then be imported into Wordperfect. Pages 490 and 491 of the Wordperfect 5.0 manual give details of the graphics programs and file formats that can be imported into the program. In fact there are many programs not mentioned in the list which are compatible with Wordperfect, because they can produce files in one of the compatible formats. For example, most CAD programs can produce HPGL files which can be imported into Wordperfect. There are file conversion programs available, and it might be possible to produce compatible files from the output of an otherwise incompatible program with the aid of one of these.

If you have a graphics program that does not support a Wordperfect compatible file format, the "screen grabber" utility provided with Wordperfect might provide a means of linking the program to Wordperfect. This program is a memory resident type, which means you run it before running the graphics program, and it then remains in the background until it is called up using the appropriate combination of key presses ("Ctrl", "Alt", and "F9" in this case).

The grabber program then temporarily takes over from the graphics program, and writes the screen image to a specified disk file in Wordperfect graphics format. There are limitations to this system, one of which is that the resolution is limited to the screen resolution. It is therefore unusable unless your computer is fitted with a graphics card, and it works best with systems that have high resolution graphics. Note that it will not work with text screens, or with some of the less common graphics cards.

It is also worth noting that it is not essential to have a computer fitted with a graphics card in order to incorporate drawings in your Wordperfect documents. On the other hand, without a graphics display it is not possible for the computer to provide a reasonable representation of the printed out page. Therefore, a computer having some graphics capability is a decided asset if you intend to make use of drawings in your Wordperfect documents. In fact a high resolution display is a great asset if you intend to make extensive use of these facilities.

As indicated on pages 490 and 491 of the Wordperfect 5.0 manual, some graphics programs produce files that can be directly imported into Wordperfect 5.0, while others produce files that must undergo a conversion process first. This conversion has to be undertaken using a separate program and is not achieved using a Wordperfect command. The conversion program is on the "CONVERSION" disk (not the "FONTS/GRAPHICS" disk), and is the file called "graphcnv.exe". I use this program by copying it to another floppy disk, together with the drawing files I wish to convert. With this disk in drive A, and drive A set as the default drive, it is then a matter of first typing "graphcnv" followed by "Return" to run the program. Then at the prompts supply the input and output file names, and leave the rest to the conversion program. You can direct the output of the program to the Wordperfect sub-directory if you are using a hard disk system, but I prefer to keep the files on floppy disk and load them from there when they are needed. Once a conversion has been made, you are taken back into the operating system. Therefore, you must re-run the program for each additional conversion that is required.

It is only fair to point out that graphics conversion processes are frequently less than 100% successful. Graphics conversion is a very complicated process, and in many cases a number of compromises have to be accepted. If you need to convert the output of a program to a popular format, and then convert this to Wordperfect format, the double conversion process increases the risk of problems. The example of Figure 3.1 was produced using Autocad, converted to its DXF file format, and then converted to Wordperfect graphics format in "graphcnv". It is inaccurate in a number of respects, the most obvious one being that the text in the caption has been stretched to the point where it goes outside the drawing's frame. Errors in text strings probably represent the most common cause of problems when undertaking graphics conversions. There is another major problem in this example in that some extra lines have appeared in the graph line part of the drawing. There is a more minor problem in that the pointed line either side of the "Time" legend has been blunted.

Wordperfect does not permit any complex editing of drawings, and so it is a matter of producing drawings that Wordperfect (and any conversion processes) can handle properly. It might take some trial and error in order to get things just right, but it is usually possible to achieve workable results. If you require a caption and a frame around a drawing, then it is probably better to add these in Wordperfect rather than including them in the original drawing.

Loading Graphics

When dealing with graphics in Wordperfect it is important to realise that it is a word processor which has the ability to import graphics into a document. It is not a true desk top publishing program, and if you try to use it as such you will probably find it rather difficult

82

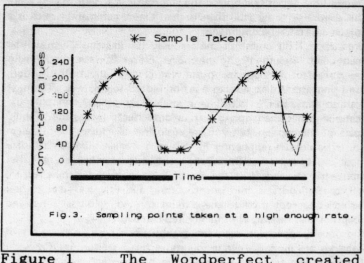

Fig.3. Sampling points taken at a high enough rate.

Figure 1 The Wordperfect created caption.

Fig.3.1 Graphics conversions are not always successful. It is generally safer to add captions and frames in Wordperfect rather than including them on the original drawing.

going. With most desk top publishing programs it is quite alright to use them on the basis of loading in graphics images, sizing them and positioning them on the page, and then loading in the text which then flows around the graphics. In fact this is the best way to use many desk top publishing programs. As Wordperfect is primarily a text processing program, it is generally better to put in all the text first, and to then add the drawings into what is in other respects a fully checked and finished document. You can still have the text flow around the drawing if necessary, which it probably will be in most cases.

The first task when placing a drawing in a document is to produce a graphics box for it. This is the area where the drawing will go in the document, and this area can be bounded by a box, or not, as required. Most of the graphics functions are, as one would expect, provided by the "Graphics" command ("Alt" plus "F9"). This brings up a list of five options on the status line, four of which are different box types (the fifth is the "Line:" command, which is a simple line drawing option).

Option 1 ("Figure;") is the one used for diagrams which will be captioned "Figure 1", "Figure 2", "Figure 3", etc., underneath each diagram. Wordperfect puts in the "Figure" part of the caption, and you are free to add to this, or indeed to delete it. The next option is "Table;", which is intended for tables, and puts the caption above the graphics box. Wordperfect supplies the "Table" part of the caption, but you are again free to add to this or delete it. The default numbering for tables is Roman numerals incidentally. Option 3 is "Text Box;", and it is intended for text that must be set apart from the rest of the document for some reason. "User Defined;" is the fourth option, and this is a graphics box which does not provide any default caption. You set it up and caption it (if necessary) in the desired manner.

Once you have chosen the graphics box type, a fresh set of options are displayed along the status line. Option 1 ("Create;") is the one to use when defining a graphics box and filling it with a graphics image. Option 2 ("Edit;") enables an existing graphics box to be edited, such as changing its contents or its position on the page. These two options operate in much the same way, but with one you start from scratch whereas with the other you operate on an existing box, drawing, and set of parameters. Another slight difference is that with the "Edit;" option you are given an opportunity to change from the default Figure/Table number, whereas the "Create;" option automatically selects the next number and takes you straight into the main graphics menu (Figure 3.2).

The first option ("Filename") is used to load in the graphics image that must occupy the graphics box. The "F5" ("List Files") command can be used here if desired. It is not essential to load anything into the box, and it can be left completely empty if desired. This may not seem to be very worthwhile, but it might be necessary to paste in a photograph or drawing on the printed out document. You might then wish to load in a rough graphics image to show what will eventually occupy that space, but the chances are that you will simply wish to leave the box completely empty. The second option ("Caption;") enables you to add to or alter the default caption. Note that some of the characteristics of the caption (its position for example) are selected using the "Options:" option mentioned previously, and can not be altered

```
Definition: Figure

    1 - Filename            GRAPH1.WPG (Graphic)

    2 - Caption             Figure 1.  A demonstation gpahics

    3 - Type                Paragraph

    4 - Vertical Position   0"

    5 - Horizontal Position Right

    6 - Size                3.25" wide x 2.14" (high)

    7 - Wrap Text Around Box Yes

    8 - Edit


Selection: 0
```

Fig.3.2   An example graphics box definition screen. Option 8 enables the drawing to be scaled rotated etc.

under the "Caption" option.

The third option permits one of three box types to be selected. Probably the "Paragraph" type is the one that will be used most often, and this is the default box type. This type of box moves with the text that flows around it, whereas the "Page" type has a fixed position on the page. With the "Character" type the graphics box is treated like a text character.

Options 4 and 5 provide control over the vertical and horizontal positions (respectively) of the graphics box. Just what effect these options have depends on the kind of graphics box selected in option 3. With the paragraph type, the position is relative to the beginning of the paragraph in which the cursor currently resides. For page type boxes it is the position relative to the top left hand corner of the page. If the box occupies a full page, then obviously these options are irrelevant. If the character type is selected, then the vertical position is restricted to aligning the text with the top, middle, or bottom of the box (the bottom of the graphics box is the default setting).

The next option ("Size"), provides three different methods of determining the size of the graphics box. With the width option you specify the required width for the box, and then Wordperfect automatically adjusts the height so that the aspect ratio of the drawing is accurately retained. The height method is much the same, except you specify the height and Wordperfect calculates the appropriate width. The third option enables the user to specify both the height and width of the box. Note that the drawing's aspect ratio will not be altered if you choose a box size that has an aspect ratio that is different to that of the drawing. The drawing will be placed in the middle of the box, with gaps above and below, or to either side, as necessary.

Probably in most cases the text will be required to automatically wrap around the box, but with option 7 you can disable this facility. Normally the box, complete with its identification number ("Fig 1", "Tab 1", etc.) is shown on the document screen, but it will not be shown if text wrapping facility is disabled. It can still be seen using the "Preview;" option of the "Print" command. If you wish to obtain a realistic impression of what the final printout will actually look like, you will need to make extensive use of the preview facility anyway.

The final option ("Edit") is an interesting one which takes you into a graphics screen which shows the graphics box and its contents.

A range of editing options are then available, but these only permit global changes to the drawing, such as rotating the image and altering its size relative to the box. Any editing of individual lines and text in the drawing must be done using the drawing program prior to loading the graphics image into Wordperfect. Fine editing of clip art is only possible if you have a suitable paint or drawing program that can be used to process images prior to loading them into Wordperfect.

Really the only way to get to grips with using graphics in Wordperfect is to load in some dummy text and then try inserting a few images into this. Try out as many options as possible and note their effect. Remember that provided your computer system has graphics capability, the preview facility can be used to give an accurate impression of what the final printout will look like, and you do not need to keep printing out pages to see what they look like.

Remember also that option "G" under the "Print" command enables you to select low, medium, or high graphics quality. Printing is likely to be much slower when printing out pages that contain graphics, especially if they contain several graphics images. Do not worry if when you tell the printer to start printing, nothing happens for a while. This is probably just a delay while the computer works out what data needs to be sent to the printer. There may well be further delays of this type during the printing process. Selecting low or medium quality printing gives quicker results when checking pages, but the better quality of the "High" option is normally required for final printouts. Even using the highest graphics quality, in absolute terms the quality might not be very good. This depends on the program used to produce the drawings, and also on the type of printer used to produce the final printouts.

If you should want to remove a graphics box from a document, the easiest way to achieve this is to use the "Reveal Codes" command to show the control code that is placing the appropriate graphics box in the document. Place the cursor on this code and then press the "Delete" key. If the graphics box is a character type, it will be shown on the screen as a block character which can be deleted in the normal way, except that you will be asked to confirm the deletion by pressing the "Y" key. Bear in mind that there is a limit of twenty graphics boxes per page.

Finally

A large percentage of Wordperfect's commands have been covered in this book, but limitations on space have resulted in some facilities not being mentioned, and others only being covered very briefly. It was not the intention for this book to be a complete guide to Wordperfect anyway. Its purpose is to first get the reader to the stage where he or she can get text into the program and get it printed out again. The aim of the rest of the book is then to enable the reader to get text properly formatted, and to cover the more useful of the more advanced features. If you can use and understand all the commands described in this publication, then you have reached the stage where you have a good understanding of the program, and you should be able to exploit its potential.

Do not overlook the fact that there are further commands at your disposal though. It is definitely worthwhile checking through the reference section of the manual to see what else the program can do. The "Macros" feature for example, is one which many advanced users of Wordperfect find can save them large amounts of time. Once you have largely mastered and got the feel of the program, learning to use the more advanced features should be reasonably straightforward.

Chapter 4

WORDPERFECT 5.1

The latest version of Wordperfect is version 5.1. This is largely compatible with earlier versions, particularly version 5.0. It mainly adds features to Wordperfect 5.0 rather than making any radical changes to the command structure. Therefore, the information provided in Chapters 1, 2 and 3 applies to version 5.1 as well as version 5.0. In this chapter we will look at some of the main additions in Wordperfect 5.1.

If you are used to earlier versions of the program, where installation on a hard disk is achieved by simply copying the relevant files from the floppy disks to the hard disk, you should note that version 5.1 is not installed in this way. There is an installation program on the "Install" disk, and you must load the program by running this and following the on-screen instructions. The installation program will find the appropriate files, including the ones that are scattered around the floppy disks, filling in the otherwise unused gaps on the disks. Compression would seem to have been applied to some of the files, and the installation program expands them back to usable files. Simply copying the compressed files to the hard disk is of no use, since they are unusable in this form.

If you are upgrading from Wordperfect 5.0 to Wordperfect 5.1 there should be no major difficulty in reading in your old files. Slight changes may occur during the automatic conversion process due to differences in fonts or some other minor differences between the two versions of the program, but any changes that occur will normally be very slight indeed. A point worth bearing in mind is that the improvements to the new version have resulted in some extra files being included, and some existing files increasing in size. Loading in the full system takes up about 4.5 megabytes of hard disk space, which is approximately 2 megabytes more than version 5.0.

Mouse Control
Undoubtedly the large addition in Wordperfect 5.1 is the mouse control it now supports. There have actually been mouse and menu programs for Wordperfect for a number of years now. I remember using such a program that was supplied with a mouse I bought

several years ago, and which was for use with version 4.1 of Word-perfect. However, with Wordperfect 5.1 the menu system and mouse control is actually built into the program, and is not in the form of a utility program which you run prior to running Word-perfect itself.

Actually, in order to utilize the mouse and menu control you must run the mouse driver before running Wordperfect. It is only fair to point out that you do not actually need a mouse in order to use the menu control system, but it is also only fair to point out that this method of control is really only at its best if you do use it in conjunction with a mouse. Here we will only consider the menus when used in conjunction with a mouse.

To bring up the menu bar at the top of the screen you must either press the "Alt" and "=" keys, or click the right mouse button. I had slight problems with first trying out Wordperfect 5.1 with a mouse, because clicking the right hand button often had no effect. The problem seems to be due to any slight movement of the mouse blocking the right mouse button. Therefore, take due care to keep the mouse still when operating this button.

Activating the menus will also cause a second cursor to appear (as will movement of the mouse). This second one is the mouse cursor, and it is easily distinguished from the ordinary cursor. The latter is a flashing underline character, while the mouse cursor is a non-flashing filled rectangle. If you move the mouse cursor to any point within a document and click the left button, the ordinary cursor will jump to the same point. This is a very quick and easy way of moving the cursor to the desired point when editing a document.

Note though, that mouse cursor can not be used to scroll the screen in the same way as the ordinary cursor. Simply trying to take the mouse cursor off the bottom of the screen will not scroll the screen. However, if you hold down the right mouse button it is then possible to scroll the screen up or down by taking the mouse cursor to the bottom or top of the screen.

Once summoned up the menu bar is not a permanent fixture incidentally. Clicking the right mouse button again removes it. Clicking the left mouse button with the mouse cursor not on the menu bar also causes the latter to disappear. In order to bring down a menu you simply position the mouse cursor on the appropriate header word in the menu bar and then click the left mouse button. Figure 4.1 shows the menu bar and the "Tools" menu. There is no

```
                        Spell          Ctrl-F2
                        Thesaurus      Alt-F1

                        Macro              ▶

                        Date Text      Shft-F5
                        Date Code      Shft-F5
                        Date Format    Shft-F5

                        Outline        Shft-F5▶
                        Paragraph Number Shft-F5
                        Define         Shft-F5

                        Merge Codes    Shft-F9▶
                        Merge          Ctrl-F9

                        Sort           Ctrl-F9

                        Line Draw      Ctrl-F3
```

Doc 1 Pg 1 Ln 1" Pos 1"

*Fig.4.1   The menu header bar at the top of the screen plus the
           "Tools" pop-down menu*

point in giving a complete list of what is available under each menu
header word. You can soon discover this by looking down each
menu in turn.

When using menus you do not really have to remember what is
available under each heading. In most cases you can look along the
header words and make an intelligent guess as to which one will
provide the desired function. For example, one could reasonably
expect "text In" to be found under the "FILE" heading. Some
functions do not really match up with a header word particularly
well. For example, there is no obvious home for the setup function,
which can actually be found under the "FILE" menu. However, it
does not take long to look down a few menus if your first guess or
guesses are wrong. You should find that you soon get used to this
method of control and quickly locate the function you require. It
is generally accepted that menu control is easier for beginners,

although experienced Wordperfect users may prefer to use the key codes.

In order to select a menu function you simply place the mouse cursor on the appropriate line of the menu and press the left mouse button. If you wish to exit from a menu without selecting a function, simply press the right mouse button. Alternatively, move the mouse cursor off the menu and press the left mouse button. If you have selected the wrong menu, move the mouse cursor over the header word for the correct menu, and press the left mouse button. This will cancel the wrong menu and bring down the correct one.

Once you have selected a function, things are much the same as if you had selected the function using the usual key press or presses. When mouse control has been selected, the normal key codes will still operate incidentally. When you are into one of the normal Wordperfect menu screens it is still possible to use the mouse to control things to some extent. In the "List Files" screen for example, you can select a file by placing the mouse cursor on the file name and pressing the left mouse button. If something like a "Yes/No" option appears on the status line at the bottom of the screen, you can select the desired option by clicking on it with the mouse. With some ordinary Wordperfect menus the mouse seems to be largely ineffective, so you really need to experiment a little to find out where the mouse can and can not be used to good effect.

Do not panic if the mouse cursor disappears when you start typing on the keyboard. It is meant to do this, so that you are left with an uncluttered screen when using the keyboard. Simply moving the mouse will cause the mouse cursor to reappear. Pressing the right mouse button results in the menu bar appearing and the mouse cursor reappearing.

A useful point to remember is that the mouse can be used to quickly block a piece of text. Place the mouse cursor at one end of the block and press the left mouse key. While still holding down the left button, move the mouse cursor to the other end of the block and then release the button. The screen should then show the correct piece of text in the blocked text colour scheme. Block operations can then be performed on this text in the usual way. When using the mouse in this way it can be used to scroll the screen, much the same as when the right hand mouse button is operated.

The setup command has been modified to accommodate mouse control. There is a "Mouse" option in the initial setup menu, and when this is selected you are taken into a menu which enables various

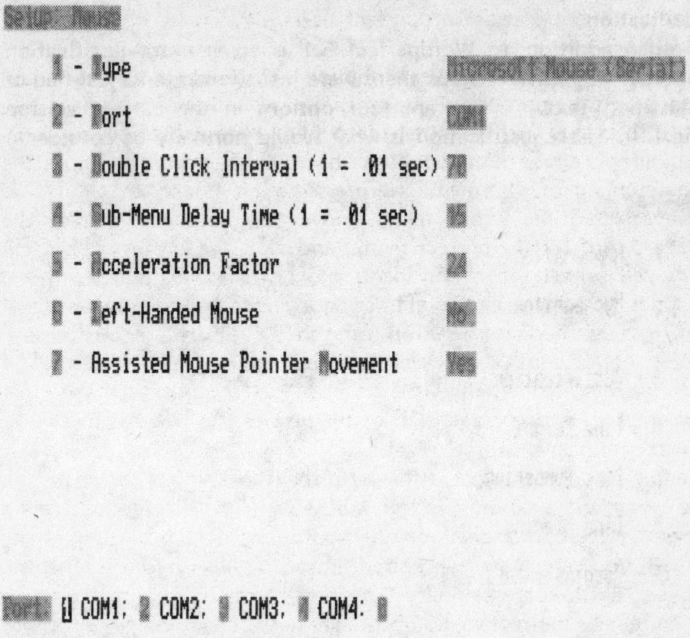

Setup: Mouse

    1 - **T**ype   Microsoft Mouse (Serial)

    2 - **P**ort   COM1

    3 - **D**ouble Click Interval (1 = .01 sec) 70

    4 - **S**ub-Menu Delay Time (1 = .01 sec)   15

    5 - **A**cceleration Factor   24

    6 - **L**eft-Handed Mouse   No

    7 - Assisted Mouse Pointer **M**ovement   Yes

Port: 1 COM1; 2 COM2; 3 COM3; 4 COM4: 0

*Fig.4.2   The mouse control menu. It is worth experimenting a little
           to get things to your liking*

mouse parameters to be set (Fig.4.2). An important category here
is the "Mouse Type". The default setting for the mouse type is
"MOUSE.COM", and this is a general setting for use with practically
any mouse. As explained previously, you must run the mouse driver
before entering Wordperfect or the mouse will not operate. If there
is an option specifically for your mouse, then having selected this
option the mouse will operate with Wordperfect without having to
first load the mouse driver program. This is dependant on the
correct port being selected from the mouse setup screen (unless a
"bus" mouse is used).

The other parameters control such things as whether the mouse
is set for left or right handed operation (left hand operation switches
the mouse button functions), and delay times. It is probably worthwhile experimenting a little with these settings to determine what
suits you best.

Justification

Another addition to Wordperfect 5.1 is some extra justification options. In earlier versions there were just two options: justified or unjustified text. There are four options in the current version (Fig.4.3). Left justification is what would normally be considered

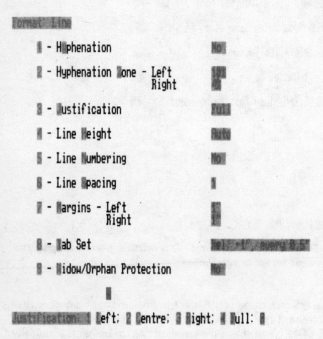

Fig.4.3   There are now more justification options available

unjustified text (i.e. neat left hand border, but a jagged right hand border). Full justification is normal justified text (i.e. added spaces to make the left and right hand borders neat). Right justification has a neat right hand border, but a jagged left hand border. Centre justification has both the left and right hand borders left rough, but every line is centred (Fig.4.4). In centre justification it is much the same as if you blocked the text and then invoked the "centre line" command. Having this available as a justification option is obviously more convenient where a large amount of text must be centred.

Operational amplifier techniques seem to dominate modern
preamplifier design. Even where preamplifiers are not built
around true operational amplifier integrated circuits, they
are usually based on specialist audio chips that are
fundamentally just operational amplifiers plus some built-in
biasing and feedback components. Preamplifiers based on
discrete circuitry are something of a rarity these days, but
even these tend to be based on what are basically operational
amplifier style circuits, complete with differential inputs.

This is really not all that surprising. Operational amplifier
techniques make it very easy to set any desired input
impedance and voltage gain figures. Unlike many other types
of audio amplifier, these figures can be set quite accurately.
Using 1% resistors, which are now availably quite cheaply, the
error in the input impedance would be no more than 1%. The
maximum error in the voltage gain would be no more than 2%.

*Fig.4.4 Some centre justified text. This is much like blocking the
text and then selecting the "centre line" option*

Help!

The help facility has been improved, and is now context sensitive.
For example, if you go into one of the main Wordperfect menus
such as the "Line" control screen, pressing the "F3" key will bring
up some information about the various facilities available. If you
were to then go on and select an option, such as "Justification" on
the "Line" control screen, pressing "F3" would then bring up some
information about the various types of justification available (Fig.
4.5).

I would have to say that most of the on-line help systems I have
encountered, including most of the context sensitive ones, seem to
be of limited practical value. The new Wordperfect help system
seems to be an exception though.

Allows you to specify how text should be aligned with respect to the left and right margins. WordPerfect inserts a code at the cursor location. If your cursor is not at the left margin when you set justification, [DSRt] is inserted before the setting. Text in the document is justified as you have indicated until you insert another code that changes the setting.

Left Align text against left margin, leaving right margin ragged.

Centre Centre text between margins. The result is similar to centring each line of text using Centre (Shft-F6). When you block lines of text and press Centre, WordPerfect inserts a [Just: Centre] code before the text and a [Just:] code after the text that returns the justification to its original setting. Should you alter justification above the centred text, you may have to manually change the [Just:] code after the centred text.

Right Align text against right margin, leave left margin ragged.

Full Align text against right and left margins. The result is the same as the Right Justification familiar to WordPerfect 5.0 users.

Selection: 0   (Press ENTER to exit Help)

Fig.4.5 One of the Wordperfect 5.1 context sensitive help screens

File Names

An interesting enhancement to Wordperfect 5.1 is the breaking of the eight character (plus three character extension) file name limit. I suppose that this is only partially true in that the files are saved on disk in an abbreviated form which conforms to the normal MS/DOS conventions. However, it is possible to enable the use of long file names by going first to the "Setup" menu, then the "Environment" sub-menu, and then the "Document Management/ Summary" sub-sub-menu. Answer "Yes" to the "Long Document Names" option.

With this option enabled it is possible to use document names of up to 68 characters in length. Furthermore, these names can include any normal characters, including those that are illegal as standard MS/DOS file names. For example, it is quite legitimate to use the space and full-stop characters in Wordperfect long document names. Something such as "Wordperfect 5.1 Book Chapter 4" would be unacceptable on a number of counts as an ordinary MS/DOS file name, but it is quite acceptable as a Wordperfect long document name.

Finally

There are other additions to Wordperfect, some of which are worthy of brief mention here. For those who are interested in using Wordperfect for the preparation of scientific or mathematical material there is an interesting addition to the graphics function. This is the ability to include equations in documents. The equation option takes you into a special editing screen where complex equations can be put together. As this is an extension of the graphics screen, the equations produced are not visible in the normal editing screen (but they can be seen on the preview screen, of course).

In a similar vein, there is a "Tables" option under the "Columns" command. This gives you what is effectively a miniature spreadsheet, which could be very useful for those involved in the production of practically any form of mathematical document.

There is a minor but useful addition to the "Shell" command. Previously you had to go out of Wordperfect and into the operating system, issue the relevant command or commands, and then type "exit" to return to Wordperfect. There is now a second option, called "DOS Command". After this option has been selected you type in the DOS command that you require. This command is then executed, after which you are placed back in Wordperfect again, without having to type "exit". This is obviously a little more convenient when only one command is needed.

For those who make use of the macro facility there are now a couple of additions. These are FOR and WHILE loops, which help to make the macro system more like a simple programming language. The "Reveal Codes" window normally occupies about half the screen. There is now a "Setup" option which enables the size of this window to be set at any desired size, which in practice means that you can make it smaller if you like. There are a few changes to the menu structure, such as the page numbering options now being controlled under a single sub-menu. However, anyone who is used to working with Wordperfect 5.0 should have no difficulty in working with version 5.1.

Index

Notes

Notes

Notes

Notes

Notes